How to collect money that is owed to you

How to collect money that is owed to you

Mel Lewis

McGRAW-HILL Book Company (UK) Limited

London · New York · St Louis · San Francisco · Auckland · Bogotá
Guatemala · Hamburg · Johannesburg · Lisbon · Madrid · Mexico
Montreal · New Delhi · Panama · Paris · San Juan · São Paulo
Singapore · Sydney · Tokyo · Toronto

Published by
McGRAW-HILL Book Company (UK) Limited
MAIDENHEAD · BERKSHIRE · ENGLAND

British Library Cataloguing in Publication Data
Lewis, Mel
How to collect money that is owed to you.
1. Corporations—Finance 2. Industrial management
I. Title
658.1′5 HG4026
ISBN 0-07-084578-6 cased
ISBN 0-07-084948-X pbk

Library of Congress Cataloging in Publication Data
Lewis, Mel.
How to collect money that is owed to you.
Bibliography: p.
Includes index.
1. Collecting of accounts. I. Title.
HG3752.5.L48 658.8′8 81-20906
ISBN 0-07-084578-6 cased AACR2
ISBN 0-07-084948-X pbk

345 CUP 887
Printed and bound in Great Britain at
The University Press, Cambridge

Contents

Preface

This book will actually help you profit from the recession. But that isn't something to feel guilty about. I'm not suggesting you make capital out of the misfortunes of others. Far from it. I say merely that the 'hard times' lessons revealed in these pages will not only help you get paid faster—from day one—but that they will also have real, lasting benefit, and must lead to greater profitability long-term for your business. Did I say 'merely'...?

For the good news is that this is a 'how to' book with a refreshing difference. It's written for the businessman or businesswoman who is also a *busy* man or woman. Unlike many other handbooks in which the Secrets of Success demand that you develop the right mental attitude, or spend years practising the author's special methods, many of the suggestions offered here can be simply copied.

You can improve your cash collection today, and it won't cost a penny more than the normal, ineffective methods of invoicing and reminder follow-ups. Other techniques mentioned will cost a minimum of cash, but are sure to repay your investment handsomely. In a few brief months you will learn how to adapt these fast pay techniques to your own particular business—and get even better paid every step of the way.*

But please don't put off the day you start. The time is right—now. And don't take my word for it. Just look at the figures. For every nine small businesses that went out of business in 1979, ten said goodbye in 1980. And last year limited companies took their worst beating ever, more winding up than ever before. Poor cash flow was a major contributing factor in many cases.

But, as I say, I appreciate that you are a busy person, with little time for reading. That's why the first chapter is a crash course in pay-up routines.

* Let me know how you get on, by the way; please send any new wrinkles you learn that you'd like to pass on, to help another businessman out of trouble. Write to me c/o my publishers, McGraw-Hill Book Company (UK) Limited, Shoppenhangers Road, Maidenhead, Berks SL6 2QL, naming the title of this book.

Preface

Read no further and you'll still be ahead of the game. Of course I hope you'll want to keep reading; and frankly, given the state of the economy, I think you owe it to yourself to keep right on to the end.

Mel Lewis

1. First steps towards getting paid on time every time

Swift payment: why you need it

Your business needs flowing cash as much as a body needs blood to live and grow. Without it, how can you replenish stocks at the best prices (by paying cash and claiming the discount)? How can you invest in new equipment; put money into research; have the confidence to take on new staff?

When people don't pay up, what happens? You are forced to borrow—dearly. To pay the interest you must charge more for your goods or services. Becoming less competitive you trade less, making it harder still to turn over and pay your own bills! For the horrid truth is: slow payment is catching.

No wonder some businesspeople turn to the cash-rich, tax-free black market—and risk losing, overnight, the reputation (not to mention the living) they have fought long hard years to build up. And the country as a whole suffers, too.

People talk about the 'spiral of slow payment.' The truth is, it is more like a black hole, sucking all into a miasma of worry, anger and commercial paralysis. But there is one vital difference. From a black hole, scientists tell us, there is no escape. From slow payment, fortunately, there is release. This book has been written with that one aim: to show *you* the way out.

Hacking away the myths about slow payment

Myth 1. Everybody suffers from it

They do. But not everybody suffers as much as you do. Take a look at some figures prepared by Dun & Bradstreet, arguably the biggest debt collection and 'business information' company in the world. They show just how sloppy payment patterns are; and some trades are much worse than others (Fig. 4.2, page 45).

A large leather and fur wholesaler waited 50 days for payment; a small manufacturer in electrical engineering waited 90 days; a large timber and furniture retailer, 100 days. But a large jewellery and precious metals wholesaler could get paid, on average, in just over one day! Clearly the jewellery buyer pays cash on the nail. Other traders have to wait for an inefficient accounting system to chug into action and spew out their cheques, often long after the due date.

Myth 2. A firm with no bad debts isn't trying hard enough

If it was thrusting out in the market place, grasping new business opportunities, it must, so the cliché goes, be taking more risks. And some of the risks would not pay off: hence the debt problem. Of course there is a nugget of truth here. But it is tempting also to work the theory backwards: 'I have bad debts, therefore I am an aggressive business opportunist whose bad luck with debts is par for the course!'

Late payment is so easily taken for granted in business. Many firms go out on a song and a prayer that customers won't give them too bad a time, that their books will somehow balance at the end of the year. But consider: the money you don't have in is, given inflation, sinking in value for every day it is past due. More, it is *not* earning interest in your bank, *nor* is it being profitably ploughed back into your business. Having too little liquid capital can harm you in other ways. You will be unable to pay quick cash and take advantage of a supplier's discount. But more: having cash in hand is so powerful a tool that many times you will be able to *create* discount opportunities (by hard bargaining) where none existed. Without cash in hand, seasonal or sudden demands may find you short—and back you crawl to the bank. Meanwhile, your debtors dine out in style—on you! It doesn't have to be this way.

Myth 3. The more you sell, the more money you make

Often, but not always. Some 'sell, sell, sell' salesmen are actually a liability to the firm that employs them. They drum up good business on paper only; getting paid later becomes more of a headache than the new trade was worth! The point was made vividly clear to me by a book which I read just before I started work on this one: *Winning Through Intimidation*, by Robert J. Ringer.

It's an American book. But don't let that put you off; the Americans have a far better reputation for getting swiftly paid than the British. And Ringer writes of his experiences as an outrageously successful real-estate salesman. But don't let that put you off either; the lessons he outlines are real and relevant to anyone in any business.

Like many of us, Ringer had read a number of the 'succeed as a salesman' books. He had worked hard at putting the authors' advice into practice; he knew plenty of other would-be go-getting salesmen who had similarly studied, and applied, the success techniques—and all (himself included) with a curious lack of success.

According to Ringer, once the flowery language of such books had been hacked away, what they appeared to be saying was that if a salesman (whom I define as anyone involved in business for profit) worked hard, long hours, if he practised and displayed a 'positive mental attitude', then he would surely succeed. The books didn't actually say when success would come; merely that 'ultimately' it must arrive.

Ringer knew many salesmen who had become excited by the language of the success books and the hope they held out; yet every day when the salesmen went out into the real world, they would continue to 'get their heads bashed in' in the jungle in which the guerrilla warfare of real-life business takes place. The promised rewards remained an elusive dream. Ringer had spotted that books on sales' techniques entirely overlooked the most important step of all in any sales strategy.

The four steps commonly set down managed to sound convincing and complete:

1. Obtain a product to sell.
2. Locate a market for the product.
3. Implement a marketing method.
4. Close the sale.

But almost always the fifth, and by far the most important, step was left out:

5. GET PAID!

Myth 4. Pushing for payment is bad for business

Being pushy surely is a mistake—in any part of life (see extract from Administration of Justice Act 1970, overleaf). But asking properly—in a thoroughly professional way—for money which is rightfully yours carries no risk.

Although you will, from time to time, seriously upset someone by asking to be paid, you will quickly discover that those who are most offended by being brought into line are those who most want to step out of line. And that type of risk you are better off without.

One of the curious benefits of acting in a forthright, professional manner when it comes to pay time, is that you stand out from the crowd. You develop a higher profile than those around you who accept their lowly, slowly paid lot. And that can work to your advantage: it can mean getting more work, more orders—just because everyone knows who you are.

And another thing; you win respect, too, for your efficiency and perseverance. Because when the game's over, it's the chips you have in your hand that count. And that's something that every businessman appreciates: even those who owe you dough.

ADMINISTRATION OF JUSTICE ACT 1970, PART V: MISCELLANEOUS PROVISIONS

Punishment for unlawful harassment of debtors.

40.—(1) A person commits an offence if, with the object of coercing another person to pay money claimed from the other as a debt due under a contract, he—

(*a*) harasses the other with demands for payment which, in respect of their frequency or the manner or occasion of making any such demand, or of any threat or publicity by which any demand is accompanied, are calculated to subject him or members of his family or household to alarm, distress or humiliation;

(*b*) falsely represents, in relation to the money claimed, that criminal proceedings lie for failure to pay it;

(*c*) falsely represents himself to be authorised in some official capacity to claim or enforce payment; or

(*d*) utters a document falsely represented by him to have some official character or purporting to have some official character which he knows it has not.

(2) A person may be guilty of an offence by virtue of subsection (1)(*a*) above if he concerts with others in the taking of such action as is described in that paragraph, notwithstanding that his own course of conduct does not by itself amount to harassment.

(3) Subsection (1)(*a*) above does not apply to anything done by a person which is reasonable (and otherwise permissible in law) for the purpose—

(*a*) of securing the discharge of an obligation due, or believed by him to be due, to himself or to persons for whom he acts, or protecting himself or them from future loss; or

(*b*) of the enforcement of any liability by legal process.

(4) A person guilty of an offence under this section shall be liable on summary conviction to a fine of not more than £100, and on a second or subsequent conviction to a fine of not more than £400.

Myth 5. Making people pay up on time is difficult and expensive

It isn't. It's often easy. And, most of the time, costs no more than the usual, inefficient accounting methods. And just in case you are so busy making money (as opposed to chasing it) that you don't have the time to stay the course (this book), here's a cameo picture of the key steps towards getting paid on time, every time.

1. Get it in writing. Because firms so often have a pecking order for payment—they pay their most important suppliers first, small fry later—it helps to come on strong from step 1. Make it clear that you will not stomach slow payment. And nothing improves your 'image', swells your stature, more than good, clear documentation.

Every deal, every alteration in specification, every renegotiation of terms or fee must go down on paper. And the more a client tells you 'We don't do business like that here'...'We do everything on a handshake'...'No one else has ever asked me to write a letter before'...'Don't you trust me?'...the more the customer smarts with every 'insult' to his 'honour' or 'integrity' your simple request for 'something on paper' incites, the more you need that piece of paper! Because it's a penny to a pound you will be led up the garden path, by the hand, when pay day draws near—if you don't get it in writing.

By the way, when someone takes great pains to reassure you of his integrity, while refusing to commit himself in writing, the best way to handle this is to listen patiently. Then say: 'So there's nothing to worry about?' The client will agree: 'Nothing!' 'So there's no reason why you can't put it in writing?'

Rarely a customer says he will put pen to paper, and even means it. But for one reason or another, he never gets round to it. Or time is too short for you to wait for a written go-ahead. Then what? Easy. You must provide your own paperwork 'evidence'.

Nothing fancy is needed. Just write as if you were talking with the client, face to face, going over your agreement: 'So we will provide 500 red, white and blue reversible widgeripoos, unboxed, but tied together at the knees. We agree to deliver these to your Ardley HQ on.... The agreed fee for this, the first of twenty monthly shipments, is to be....' And so on.

2. Getting it in writing is sometimes not enough. Safer still is to use recorded-delivery post. (Advice of delivery post will also tell you, for sure, that your message actually arrived.) And always mark your letter that it is 'RECORDED DELIVERY'—I go into the reasons for this later.

3. State your terms clearly. Sometimes, amazingly, it's the trader's own fault he isn't paid on time. Customers, accused of abusing terms, complain: 'We don't even know when we should pay!' because terms are left off the invoice, or they are unclear. Here's what I mean. Many UK businesses state their terms as 'net monthly.' But what does this mean? It could mean payment is due:

— One month from date of despatch of goods.
— One month after the invoice date.
— One month after the goods have arrived.
— One month after the end of the month in which the goods were invoiced or sent out.

No wonder there's confusion!

Whenever you want to be paid, *spell it out* and in plain English. For example: 'Payment to be *received* within one month of invoice date above.' Better still, repeat the date alongside, in brackets.

And if your business is small and sends out hand-typed invoices for each transaction, then why not write in the actual date you want to be paid by—e.g., 'Payment to be received by 31 August 1982'?

4. Get the strength of the trade protection associations around you. Their presence, in the background, will actually help you win battles you don't even know you're fighting. For often the mere hint that you belong to a trade protection association will put the wind up a potential defaulter. He'll assume, quite rightly, that his tardiness with your cheques could quickly become common knowledge among your fellow traders. And he'll have a job doing business in the future at all!

British Mercantile Group of Companies in Sidcup, Kent, specializes in protecting the paper, stationery, pharmaceuticals, photographic and grocery trades, among others. They offer account collection (home and export), legal help, telephone collection training, and more. On pages 126–128, there is a list of helpful organizations to enable you to find the trade association that could help your business.

Another way to imply that you are 'under the wing' of an association is to join the Credit Protection Association, Acton, London, and use their 'beady eye' stickers (see Figure 1.1). These state:

Figure 1.1

5. Professional collection agencies have a very good track record for getting owed money in fast. Their cold and dispassionate third-party status chills the debtor into paying up—or so it is said. Now there's a new idea that enables any trader to mimic that effect without getting expensively tied up with any one agency.

If you are owed cash you simply buy dunning letters that *look* like those the agencies issue. The frosty, formal look, and the awesome red printed 'Final notice' can work wonders. Such letters can be bought from Global

Credit Management, Edgware, Middlesex. The more you buy, the cheaper they get.

How to win with words

You don't need me to tell you that the way you talk to people in business matters. Undeniably, most people are better talkers than they are writers; we've had more practice at it. But business people also have to put pen to paper. Sadly, most people, business or otherwise, can't be told anything—but business people especially, and those who have tasted success most of all, are among the most unteachable. This is just one of those facts of life which I don't intend to justify because there isn't time or room in this slim volume. Nor do I intend to include a thesis on 'How to write'. (By the way, the best book ever written on writing is *The Way to Write*, by Rudolf Flesch and A. H. Lass, McGraw-Hill, New York, 1947, also successfully republished in paperback as *A New Guide to Better Writing*—which just goes to prove the power of words!) But I am going to offer just one or two linguistic titbits for you to ponder. The first couple are suggested by Robert J. Ringer, author of the best-seller *Winning Through Intimidation*. Having got his fingers burned several times, it became clear to Ringer that at the start of a real-estate deal it was essential to get the seller to sign a contract guaranteeing that in the event of a successful sale he, Ringer, would get his agreed fee. Ringer also knew that producing a piece of paper called a 'Contract' would be asking to be shown the door. Quite simply, a contract *sounds* binding, menacing. So Ringer always referred to his contract as an 'understanding'. To enhance further the illusion of the 'understanding' being a casual, harmless piece of paper, Ringer didn't get a lawyer to 'draw up' his contracts—with all that awe- and fear-inspiring mumbo-jumbo lawyers favour. Instead, he wrote his 'understandings' himself, in everyday language. His easy-to-understand 'understandings' meant the same; and even if they didn't read like Doomsday documents, they still carried the same legal weight.

Another Ringer revelation came at the close of a typical deal. Invariably, there were last-minute problems, almost always aggravated, if not caused, by the seller's deal-killing lawyer. Although every business deal has 'problems', Ringer concluded that calling a problem a 'problem' was asking for more problems. It was an upsetting word: it sounded like time-consuming trouble. So he dropped it from his working vocabulary, replacing it with a blander word, 'points.'

As the client's deal-killing lawyer produced his deal-killing problems willy nilly at the closing—the short strokes part of the deal—Ringer would thank the lawyer for bringing up the 'darn good points' he had uncovered, and would then proceed to state, rather than ask, how 'we', not just the client's lawyer, 'would' (in preference to 'could') 'handle' (never 'solve') the 'point' (not 'problem').

Be a better letter writer

Most British business correspondence is appalling—dull, boring, cliché-ridden. But most of all, unfriendly and remote. The Americans are far and away better letter-writers. Here's a typical one.

Dear Mr Rickenbacker

A line of credit has been opened in your name, and with it go our very best wishes for a happy and prosperous Easter.

Saying 'hello' to a new retailer is always a happy experience for me. I intend to do everything possible to help you profit from our relationship; and that's not all. I'm confident we will become, more than just your suppliers, but your friend, too.

An easy way to start winning extra income is yours for the asking—by taking advantage of our substantial discount terms...

The easiest way to get your letters sounding chattier is to talk on to paper. Ask yourself this: what would you *say* to the person you're writing to if he were in the room. Write it down, rough as you like, and with contractions, like 'I'll' and 'don't.' Then work it over, with a pen, until it reads right. PS 'Talking' letters is also a great way of rolling aside a writer's block!

Cut the cackle when you write. Silence isn't golden in business; brevity is. Keep sentences and paragraphs short. Studies have shown that the parts of a letter that get the closest attention are the first and last paragraphs and the PS. Use that fact to get your own most urgent messages across. Don't be afraid to repeat yourself. One famous speaker got up to speak and launched into the following spiel of seminal importance: 'First,' he said, 'I'm going to tell you what I'm going to tell you. Then I'm going to tell it to you. And then I'm going to tell you what I've told you.' If you want something to sink in, say it again, Sam. If you've got anything worth saying, it'll bear a little repetition.

Musts to avoid

Avoid long-winded, hackneyed expressions. You would think that by now everyone had seen, or been told about, the section in the magazine *Private Eye* in which readers are asked to send in cuttings (usually from sociological publications) which use that laughably ponderous expression, 'ongoing situation' or just 'situation'. Still the words crop up in letters and articles with deadpan seriousness. At *The Times*, a pet hate of the sub-editors is the expression 'in the field of.' To many writers a man isn't 'a computer scientist,' he is 'an expert in the field of computer science.'

'At this moment in time' is another phrase that occurs with sick-making regularity on TV, radio and in the papers. 'Now' does just as well. Why do people use these tedious catchphrases? I don't know. I think it's because the ability to speak at length, without pausing, is a highly rated skill in western civilization. Also, it gives conversation an illusion of importance. Consider ditching all the left-hand expressions that follow, in favour of those on the right:

We acknowledge receipt of	Thank you for
Is not in a position to	Cannot
May rest assured	May be sure
Under separate cover	Separately
Advise us as to	Let us know
The undersigned	I or me
In lieu of	In place of
Pertaining to	About
In the event that	If
At which time	When
It is our understanding that	We understand
Inadvertently	Unintentionally
Along the lines of	About
We are of the opinion that	We believe
In view of the fact	Since
In the near future	Promptly or soon
Ultimo	Of last month
Proximo	Of next month
Give consideration to	Consider
In the amount of	For
We would like you to	Please
With reference to	This or these
The said application	Application
Consensus of opinion	Consensus
In connection with	About
With regard to	Concerning
We are returning herewith	We enclose
Pending receipt of	Until
With respect to	Concerning
Be so kind as to	Will you please
At this moment in time	Now
At the present time	Now

'You' is more important than you think

Whom do you put first in this world, business or otherwise? A single man or woman might, with hand on heart, be able to say 'Mum'. But for most people, No. 1 comes first. It's natural. Just as, for a family man or woman, it would be normal to put wife or husband and children first. So 'you'—and 'yours'—are a pretty high priority. Similarly in business, you will put first your own interests and those of your company. And you would expect those with whom you deal to do the same? You'd be right! They do. Then why not appeal to that sense of self at every turn? Not only should you emphasize the benefit for the other party in every business letter, but you should bring in those most riveting words, 'You' and 'Yours', as early on as possible. They will guarantee you a spellbound audience. Here are some examples:

Your orders for our goods....
You have been paying....
Your welcomed first order....
Your outstanding balance....

How to catch the customer's eye

Have you ever registered the jarring effect of reading the same word twice in a piece of prose? Usually it has been included the second time in error. You can make use of that visual hiccup effect in your own business correspondence: 'So we can fully expect to receive your cheque for full payment sent today today by First-Class Post?' The recipient will never know whether you meant the stereo effect or whether it was an accident. Never mind: it made him sit up.

First get a good typewriter

Lastly, always *type* your letters. Most handwriting is horrific. One glance, and the last thing I want to do is read anyone's handwriting. So I don't. I put it in my 'Eventually' file. And when you do type, use a good typewriter. I thought a really smart typewriter would be far too expensive—until I saw a shop-window advertisement card for an IBM Executive for a mere £48. Never mind that the machine is bright pink and big as a bus; its type-face looks like a million dollars.

By the way, the real reason why every small businessman without a secretary needs an electric typewriter is because an electric machine hides the fact that he isn't a trained typist. However hard or soft the keys are depressed, the impact of the arm (or golfball) is constant. It's the uneven pressure recorded by a manual machine that makes a beginner's work look amateurish. And when it comes to getting paid, the last thing you want to look is amateurish.

2. Why people don't pay up

So often a business writer or collection-agency spokesman will get on his high horse and hold forth on the 'immorality' of being a debtor, the upshot of which is that people who owe money should pay up because they ought to. No one forced them to take the goods which led to the debt; they are 'stealing' credit, possibly fomenting a chain reaction of slow payment and eventual business failure for some creditors, and so on. Convincing as such arguments are, they should serve only to strengthen a creditor in his resolve to get back his money—and the sooner the better. For the fact remains that people do enter agreements and then, either by intention or mishap, fail to complete according to contract. Right is on the creditor's side every time, but the reality is that collecting past dues is a continuing time-, energy- and cash-consuming preoccupation.

A little encouragement goes a long way

Accepting reality, however, is only part of the lesson. The most important next step is to *act* realistically. One of the reasons people don't pay up on time is because it pays them to keep hold of a creditor's money. For as long as it is cheaper not to pay bills than to take a bank overdraft there are sure to be slow payers. The longer a debtor can hold back from paying up, the more the money earns in his own bank account. A fairly obvious remedy, you would think, would be to offer a cash inducement to a debtor to pay up on time or sooner. Yet discounts for early payment—widely practised in America—are in an embryonic stage in the UK; and never mind that they are said to be frequently abused—i.e., taken even when paying late—the fact remains: few UK firms have even tried.

Debtors' psychology: or how to make a Freudian pay slip

An Italian expert in psychology divided debtors into four main types: impulsive buyers; people who cannot attend to detail; dreamers up of grandiose and costly schemes; those who have a careless attitude to their work.

Impulsive buyers are more likely to be found in consumer credit than in trade credit. Those who genuinely find it hard to attend to detail can be 'encouraged' to concentrate by a skilled and determined creditor, as can the slapdash debtors. The real problem indicated here are the business 'dreamers' who buy more than they can realistically handle; or are actually encouraged by sell, sell, sell salesmen to buy more than they can comfortably sell on. A salesman on commission is always a potential liability in this direction, and any overlarge order must always be viewed with suspicion and leading questions asked about the customer's trading capacity.

Much as the psychological approach has its charms, however, it is the *business* approach to debts that will bear the most fruit for the businessman. Nevertheless, a certain intuitive 'feel' for the game is essential. The creditor has to become a sort of 'debt doctor.' Much as a real medical practitioner has to differentiate between symptoms (what the patient tells him are the distinguishing features of his condition) and signs (what the doctor himself establishes and records), so the creditor has to separate the broke from the merely lame and the out-and-out monetary malingerers.

Debtors try all sorts of gambits in a bid to avoid paying up. These are just a few, ranging from the could-be factual to the downright fanciful:

1. Your cheque's in the post.
2. We've lost your invoice.
3. You didn't quote your order number/our requisition number.
4. We didn't receive the goods.
5. The goods weren't 'right.'
6. Your invoice failed to take account of a credit that's outstanding.
7. You have added on the discount we took (out of terms) on our last order.
8. The person who signs the cheque is ill/on holiday/playing golf.
9. One of the three cheque signatories is ill/on holiday/playing golf.
10. Our computer has broken down/is being reprogrammed.
11. We are being taken over.
12. An annual stocktaking is in progress.
13. It is the end of the financial year.
14. Our accounts are with the accountant.
15. Your invoice has been passed for payment, but the accountant is with the boss's secretary in the Cayman Islands.

The actual reasons for debtor delinquency are fewer in number and probably deserve mention in the following order of importance:

1. The debtor doesn't understand your terms.
2. He means well, has great business flair. But he hasn't got enough cash.
3. He's doing all right but his books are in a mess.

4. He's discovered that time is money. So he's buying some—with your money.
5. He's too busy with his own business to bother about your business.

The 'Help me, I'm in trouble' debtor

What do you do if one of your customers asks for help with paying his account? The customer who *asks* for extended credit elicits sympathy; but does he deserve it? If he took French leave of your due date first and then sought permission, possibly not. But a request received in good time, on paper, and from a principal, may merit serious consideration. These are some of the questions that will need to be answered, before help should be offered:

Is he an established customer?
Is he historically a reliable payer?
What effect will there be on your cash flow if he is granted new terms?
What amount of money is at stake?
How much more credit does he want and over what period?
How will your credit risk be affected?
Is his business financially sound?
How much interest should you charge?
Will he pay your 'fee' as interest?
Is there some benefit for you over and above the cash you'll get?
Why is the extra credit needed?
Is there a problem in the debtor's industry generally?
Why isn't cash help forthcoming from the debtor's bank?
Is any other supplier being asked to help?
What will happen if you don't respond to his plea?

Working backwards through the questions, the last one may be the most worrying. The customer who is turned down may decide to take his trade elsewhere out of pique, something you would not wish to happen to a valued and trusted client with a long history of on-time payment. A refusal could also precipitate the demise of the client's business, in which case you'll sing long for your supper; extending credit may be the easiest course. The customer may say that all of his suppliers have been asked to extend their terms in order that he, the customer, can stock up now in anticipation of an upturn in demand towards the end of the year. You might then be wise to investigate whether others have in fact been approached, and what their reaction is.

Any credit-granting business is acting as a finance house or bank; this is normal practice. But a sound business that suddenly finds itself in trouble normally gets a positive response from a bank manager, and it would be prudent to discover why the bank has not been propositioned now or why it has refused help. A slump in the debtor's industry generally will help explain his coming to you for mercy. But you need to be sure that the slumped company you're trading with will one day, soon, walk straight again.

Why the money is needed is, these days, the least interesting or important part of the dilemma. Bank managers used to take a particularly paternalistic/moralistic attitude to why their customers wanted to borrow money. Now they just make sure the collateral is right and the payment sums make sense.

But, for the record, these are some typical on-paper reasons prospective slow payers offer:

While a major reconstruction of the company is underway, could you see your way clear to....

Our trade in Wallaguloland has suffered a severe setback recently with the changing political climate; however, the new regime has already shown itself to be more than receptive and for a short period we are wondering if....

If, in these difficult times, one cannot turn to established trading partners for help then it would be a sorry day indeed. In this respect we have been contacting our most trusted suppliers with a view to....

As you must know, S. Harp Traders, although newcomers to the field, have already established themselves as a force to be reckoned with. Much as we would regret having to transfer business from your goodselves to a virtual stripling company, nevertheless their competitive terms are such that....

The real reason for the extended credit request may never be known. In fiction books, truth will out. In business (real life) it mostly won't; besides which, the truth, in many cases, is usually irrelevant: *business* considerations are what ultimately must matter to you.

Heaven forbid that you should take advantage of a client who's down on his luck, but in business there are no prizes for being a Good Samaritan. In business, the Good Samaritan is just as likely to get his teeth kicked in, financially speaking, as he stoops to help. Yet there may be some benefit for the *Smart* Samaritan who can pull a preferential deal out of this temporary setback of his old and trusted client.

Or it may come to filthy lucre only. Are your terms acceptable, legal and not extortionate; do they take full account of the falling value of inflated money (see Figure 2.1), your administrative costs, greater risk, etc.; and does the client accept your terms? If he does accept them, will he be able to pay at the end of the day? Is the business financially strong? You may want to see up-to-date trading figures, say the last three months' accounts. You don't need to be an actuary to work out the amount of increased risk incumbent upon granting extra credit. You need to be clairvoyant. But an old Isle of Dogs' saw may be apropos here. It runs, 'When in daht, leave it aht.'

	Cumulative costs for overdue period of					
	1 month	2 months	3 months	6 months	9 months	12 months
Financing, based on an annual interest rate of 20%	£16.67	£33.61	£50.84	£104.26	£160.39	£219.38
Accounting overheads and communication costs—letters, 'phone calls, personal visits, assuming £10 per month	£10.00	£20.00	£30.00	No further communication with debtor: £30.00	£30.00	£30.00
Reduced purchasing power of £1000—caused by 10% inflation	£8.33	£16.73	£25.20	£51.04	£77.54	£104.70
Total cost	£35.00	£70.34	£106.04	£185.30	£267.93	£354.08
Agency fee @ 6% upon successful collection			£60.00			
REAL COST			£166.04			

Debt recovered through agency after three months: net gain = £1000 − £166.04 = £833.96
Debt written off after 12 months : net loss = £1000 + £354.08 = £1354.08

Figure 2.1 Cost of delayed recovery of debt, based upon a single debt of £1000 (interest and inflation calculated monthly). Reproduced by permission of Dun & Bradstreet Ltd

The period of extra credit requested may be in the order of another 30 to 60 days, the lengthened terms to stand for six or nine months. How will this affect your own cash flow? Lacking in cash, you may be unable to take advantage of a deal that suddenly materializes or have to forego a discount for lack of liquid capital.

Perhaps your best guide to the probity of a customer is his track record; and that is to be found not on his lips or those of his other suppliers, but in your own books. How he has paid you in the past says more about your client than any other testimonial.

3. Money sense for thoughtful and hopeful beginners

Offering credit enables a customer to buy greater quantity with greater confidence because he has a longer period in which to conclude his own sale. Also, it enables you to support traders who have real business flair but not much capital. Alternatively, you may want to offer credit to a firm that has sound assets but is lacking in cash.

Giving too much credit is asking for trouble. A debtor who finds a soft target in you will use the funds earmarked to pay you to pay a less lenient creditor.

Too much credit can also lead to overtrading, which can quickly lead to failure. It's a surprising fact that most firms that go under do so through incompetence, not because they are crooked.

With longer credit periods a customer may be able to keep buying even though he is over his credit limit. Take a £1000 rated customer. His £1000 December bill is due to be paid by 15 January. But he can take more goods early in January and with some firms will still not be over his limit, because he is good for £1000 a month and the mid-month payment is anticipated.

But what if this payment is not made in January or February? That customer can quickly soar beyond his original rating and become a danger to the company that lets him get away with it and also to himself.

The solution is either to cut the terms, or never let the *total* number of bills outstanding go higher than the credit rating. Or investigate the client's credit standing more thoroughly; thus, a customer wanting £1000 of credit would be vetted for his ability to pay bills of £2000.

How much credit should you give?

A customer good for £500 can buy £3000 a year on monthly terms. If he is on weekly terms he can buy £25000 worth of goods. A customer good for £10000 could be offered any of the following schemes:

1. £10000 for 7 days.
2. £5000 monthly.
3. £2500 three-monthly.

Trade credit

An accurate assessment of credit limit is vital; so, too, is the choice of payment terms. The right choice can enhance turnover and cashflow. With net monthly terms a customer rated at £5000 will be able to spend no more than £30000 annually since his cut-off point is reached after only two months. Would a significant improvement be possible if he was offered a 1 per cent discount as incentive to accept half-monthly credit?

Look at Tables 3.1 and 3.2. Over the same period cash flow improves 150 per cent. Sales double. Net profit is up 2 per cent and almost doubled—from £525 to £900, after the discount is subtracted.

Table 3.1

Month	*Week*	*Sales value in £s*	*Payment in £s*	*Balance*
1	1	625		625
	2	625		1250
	3	625		1875
	4	625		2500
2	5	625		3125
	6	625		3750
	7	625		4375
	8	625		5000
		Payment made	2500	2500
3	9	625		3125
	10	625		3750
	11	625		4375
	12	625		5000
		Payment made	2500	2500

Three months' sales = £7500
Cash flow = £5000
Net profit at 7% = £525

The truth about terms

An enormous amount has been said about trade terms. The theory is fascinating, the facts farcical. How does the following square with your own experience? Terms are:

Frequently misunderstood.
Often abused.
Sometimes not stated.
Varied as part of a deal.

Table 3.2

Month	*Week*	*Sales value in £s*	*Payment in £s*	*Balance*
1	1	1250		1250
	2	1250		2500
	3	1250		3750
	4	1250		5000
		Payment made	2500	2500
2	5	1250		3750
	6	1250		5000
		Payment made	2500	2500
	7	1250		3750
	8	1250		5000
		Payment made	2500	2500
3	9	1250		3750
	10	1250		5000
		Payment made	2500	2500
	11	1250		3750
	12	1250		5000
		Payment made	2500	2500

Three months' sales	= £15000
Cash flow	= £12000
Net profit at 7%	= £1050
Less 1% discount	= £150
Net profit after discount	= £900

Interpreted (by you) according to the importance/buying power—or year of Rolls—of the customer.

Why offer credit terms at all? The reasons commonly offered are:

1. Everyone else does.
2. The customers expect it.
3. It helps a customer take more goods to sell on.
4. Given the state of the post and the normal sales ledger department, it may make sense to call almost any transaction '10 days net' at least, and make it sound like a free gift in the form of extended credit, because it will take that long for even a return-of-post account to be settled and a record of payment made.

The truth is, choice of terms should be guided by: the normal practice in your trade; the working capital available to finance debtors; the degree of risk thought acceptable (for more risk give less credit); the nature of the goods; size of the order.

In order to maintain credibility, never trade on terms, it is said. Better to drop the price rather than lengthen the offered credit period—no matter how sensible the mathematics appear; for psychologically you could lose out. Once the customer learns how readily *you* take liberties with your terms, *he* may be tempted to follow suit!

Make terms work to your advantage

Not only should you state your terms, therefore, but you should also *spell them out* in simple language. State clearly how payment should be made, in what form, to whom and at what address. Consider penalties for slow payment in the form of interest charges, and discounts to help your cash flow.

Most UK businesses state that their terms are net monthly. But what does this mean? It could mean payment is due:

One month from date of despatch.
One month from date of invoice.
One month from arrival of goods.
One month after the end of the month in which goods were invoiced or despatched.
One month after an agreed date in the month of invoicing. (In the carpet trade, debts are expected to be settled by the 20th of the month following month of delivery.)

Always state clearly from which date the discount countdown begins.

Payment terms should be firmly included in an estimate; they should be repeated as often as possible—on headed stationery, invoice, statements. A clear statement of terms helps establish credibility early on, when it matters.

An invoice recently sent to me points up the terms and dating problems of invoices. The invoice carried no mention of terms so I sat on it. Just before a month after the invoice date I received a statement. The statement could easily have been filed as a carbon copy reminder, without a second glance. That must be the fate of many an invoice copied up and labelled 'Statement'. But as I was writing this book I gave it some attention.

It gave a 'Total now outstanding', and '*Terms*—Cash within one month of invoice' had suddenly materialized at the foot of the page. The terms should have featured large on the original document, the invoice. And although I am, in law, said to have accepted the terms of this supplier from the fact of having ordered his service and his having accepted the order, still he might have to prove precisely what his terms were. I could keep him waiting 90 days, claiming that this was normal in my trade. He might have to show proof that in his business it was one month and this was *his* normal practice. How much simpler to spell out terms in the beginning.

Another point. Suppose such a supplier had spelt out his terms. *When* should you send the money? In order to arrive on time for his 30- or 31-day slot, presumably. But you, or your paying department, might have to start thinking about that several days before due date, to get that invoice in front of them, the cheque made out and into a first-class stamped envelope. Even earlier if, very sensibly, you planned on using second-class postage. How much sooner does a big company need to set the payment ball rolling? It's no surprise that in these circumstances a cheque gets, at best, *posted* on the due date. And that can mean a week or 10 days' extra credit—especially if a week-end or a bank holiday needs to be crossed. So, if you want your bills paid by such and such a date, spell it out: 'Payment to arrive on or before....'

With so many different terms available, it helps to look through the range, see what they mean, and pick the ones that maybe could help *you* do better business.

Net. Means payment on delivery. But
Net 7, *Net 10*, etc., indicates payment in 7, 10 days, etc.

The most common UK terms appear to be:

Net monthly. The settlement for one month's deliveries, or one month's invoices, is due at the end of the following month (or before). In the United States this is known as EOM—end of month—terms. The Americans believe EOM is subject to serious abuse. The temptation is for a company to offer an apparently bona fide excuse for non-payment of deliveries/invoices that fall in the 25th-to-end-of-month period.

The standard catechism is that the new computerized accounting system has a cut-off date that effectively chops off the last week of the month from the records of that month and carries it into the next month. Genuine the excuse may be; it's also a neat method of gaining up to 38 days' extra credit.

1MO terms require payment of a full month's supplies by a specified date in the following month, generally the 7th, 10th, 15th, 25th or the last working day.

2MO terms are as above, but with an extra month's credit added; similarly 3MO, and so on.

The Americans appreciate, better than the British, that strict adherence to terms is good for business. It means business turns over more times a year and liquidity is better. They also typically operate on shorter credit, 45 days being average. In the UK, in the late 1970s, it was 70 days for a typical manufacturing company. Germany, Holland, Sweden, Belgium and Switzerland fared better, at 60 days, whereas Italy and Spain were 90-day payers.

Net 30 days. This is typical US-style payment terms. It gives an average of 15 days faster payment than net monthly.

Proximo terms. Indicates payment is to be made next month. Common terminology in grocery trade and automotive trades in America.

Weekly credit. All goods supplied between Monday and Sunday (or some other seven-day span) to be paid by a specified day the following week.

Pro forma. Commonly thought to be a 'no risk' payment method. But as this could mean either cash with order or cash before shipment there is the possibility of confusion. Why not say what you mean in plain English?

Cash with order. The harshest terms of all. No work, selection of goods, or packaging is done until the money arrives. Sometimes abbreviated to CWO or CBD, cash before delivery.

Cash before shipment. Marginally less stringent than cash with order. This may entail manufacturing goods to customer specifications while the cash is awaited. Asking for a deposit with cash before shipment is a good idea, and clearing the balance cheque before despatch is essential.

CIA, cash in advance, and Cash on advice of availability are similar to above.

Half and half. Anyone who has ever asked for an unsecured loan from a bank will appreciate the 'fair play' appeal of this approach to payment. The bank manager offers as much cash as you put up.

The thinking seems to be that a man who can find £*x* now will be able to lay his hands on £*x* later—especially once he has sold the goods for profit. A further advantage is that half and half discourages crooks, who want to not pay for 100 per cent of your goods, and conscientious debtors, who want to keep you waiting as long as possible without parting with a penny.

Stage payments. These are common where there is a long delivery period or long manufacture with big capital outlay. Plant and heavy machinery are typically the subject of stage payments; 10 or 30 per cent down and the balance on delivery or in agreed increments.

Cash terms. There is no discount option but often the opportunity to 'Examine FREE for 10 days' or some such sales tickler. There is the risk that the customer will keep the goods and not pay; return them damaged; be genuinely unsatisfied and return them unused. This approach notoriously attracts 'curiosity seekers' with no intention of buying.

COD. Cash on delivery. If the goods are not accepted, the supplier has to pay carriage both ways, plus the cost of packing. There is the additional risk of loss or damage in transit and possible insurance fee. If the goods are in short supply, a non-sale may also mean another customer has had to be turned down while the goods were, fruitlessly, out of circulation. Paradoxically, even COD deliveries imply some measure of credit, because time will elapse before the goods are sent out and the money returned and cleared if in cheque form.

AOG and *ROG* stand for arrival of goods and receipt of goods. The terms are used in the context of a discount option or end-of-the-month net payment (e.g., 2/10/EOM—2 per cent discount if paid in 10 days, 30 days net). It indicates that the discount may be taken from receipt of goods. But if the discount option is not taken up the countdown for net payment starts from the date of shipment. However, the actual date of arrival of goods is hard to monitor; the customer is somewhat on his honour here, and abuse, in the form of discounts taken late, is common.

Load over load; similar to *CND, cash next delivery.* Common in the petrol business. A tanker arrives with a fresh supply of petrol, but the tanks are not filled until the previous consignment is paid for.

Journey terms. Indicates that the rep or van salesman is to be paid.

Working to present credit limit. Normally it is considered unwise to discuss a customer's rating with him. In this pay plan, full and frank discussions are turned into a virtue. If a trusted customer of long standing is good for £5000 for 60 days and exceeds his limit after 45 days he is allowed to pay in an amount to reduce the account and so keep ordering.

Contra terms. The supplier is also a customer. For example, a supplier of raw materials sells them to a factory which processes them into a consumer product. The supplier buys the made-up article from the factory, and it is the supplier, not the factory, that sells the finished product to the public. Such credit is fraught with complications, and demands the attention of a good accountant or lawyer. Frequent settlements and reconciliations are a must.

Discounts

Discounts are losing popularity in the UK at present (whereas there is a growing tendency to charge interest on late payments). The great problem is that cheeky customers tend to take discounts and pay late as well. One trader, in his conditions of sale, states that discounts taken out of terms will be left on the account as a balance outstanding. This may help cure delinquent discount takers—or the stolen discount may never get paid.

In America discounts are far more commonly offered and taken. Indeed, not taking a discount is looked on with some suspicion. The implication seems to be that discount-takers are creditworthy bank borrowers. They use borrowed funds to take the often very good discounts offered. Those who pass up the discount must lack the credit status to go to the banks—or so the theory goes. Common US terms are 1 or 2 per cent in 10 days, with the option of paying net 30 days.

Points in favour of granting discounts include:

1. The lessened cost of collecting past due debts, counted in the form of office space, office equipment, staff salaries, postage, professional collection fees (agency fees, legal fees).
2. Never overlook, too, the worry burden of late payers. It isn't only mental and it isn't only physical angst that debtors cause: it's a bit of both. It's precisely the sort of energy that gets used up in collecting debts that is better used to create fresh business opportunities.
3. People are notoriously eager to get something for nothing. This element in the discount offer could well clinch a sale that could not otherwise be made.
4. The longer the money is outstanding, the greater the risk. A discount lessens this risk.
5. Discounts are particularly suitable for high-risk—perishable or seasonal—goods.

Discounts for payment within specified periods—7, 10 and 14 days—can range from 2½ per cent to 5 or even 6 per cent. This is commonly found where there is:

1. A large turnover.
2. Limited credit standing.
3. The customer's sale will be for quick cash.

Creative use of discounts

The value of the goods must be taken into account when offering a discount. From time to time I offer a syndicated articles column. My costs are marketing, advertising, post and secretarial; the product is words on pieces of paper; the actual product is photocopied stationery. As often as not, the time spent creating those words is already handsomely paid for from past sales. So I can afford to offer either free articles or a cash discount as an incentive. Quarterly or monthly publishers use articles rarely, so they take the cash-off terms. Weekly publications take the free articles. I prefer the latter, for the reasons given. But it's good business to offer a choice.

And as a further sweetener, to pull in the orders, I offer both free articles *and* a cash-off bonus if an order is placed in so many days.

In mail-order operations the first sale is often made as a loss leader—a loss is expected on overall costs. The second and subsequent sales make the profit, because they are made as reorders or from a catalogue with no further prompting from the company, so saving on expensive advertising. Attractive initial discounts could well pull in enough customers, as long-term sales prospects, more than to pay for the early lack of revenue.

Advertising agencies survive on the discounts they receive from advertisements they place on behalf of clients. The media have a neat method of bringing late-paying agencies into line. If the agencies don't stump up the funds to pay for their space or time, as per terms, they forfeit their 15 per cent 'kick-back.'

What is a discount worth to you?

The mistake is sometimes made of confusing the 1, 2 or $2\frac{1}{2}$ (or more) per cent discounts offered with annual percentage rates. An apparently diminutive percentage can represent a substantial percentage saving worked out on an annual basis. You need to look at what is actually being offered.

Suppose XYZ Ltd sell ABC Ltd goods to the value of £1000 on 15 January. XYZ Ltd says, 'Pay me by 15 February and take a 2 per cent discount.' What benefit is XYZ Ltd offering in yearly terms?

From the point of view of XYZ Ltd, the calculation may go like this. ABC Ltd could pay as late as March. It would not necessarily lead to loss of confidence, trade sanctions or revised credit rating. ABC Ltd could get away with it. So the discount is being offered for payment a month and a half early (mid February until end March). On a yearly basis:

$$\frac{12}{1\frac{1}{2}} \times 2\% = 16\%$$

ABC Ltd could look at the deal in a somewhat different way. They could ask themselves: 'What are we being asked to pay out, assuming we take the discount?'

$$£1000 \times 98\% = £980$$

ABC Ltd then ask themselves the question: 'Can we get a better return than £20 on our £980 over one and a half months?' The value of the discount, over a year, worked out along these lines is:

$$\frac{20}{980} \times \frac{100}{1} \times \frac{12}{1\frac{1}{2}} = 16.33\%$$

Can ABC Ltd get a better return than 16.33 per cent? If not, and there is cash in hand, they should pay the bill early and take the discount.

Checklist of points to consider when deciding on terms

1. Current practice.
2. Strength of competition.
3. Saleability of the product. Perishables are traditionally subject to shorter credit periods.
4. Margin of profit.
5. Current demand.
6. Size of order.
7. Location of customer (a customer 1000 miles away will not be able to pay seven-day bills on time).
8. Your financial position.
9. Credit rating of customer.

The lower the level of profit, the more important it is to get your clients to stick to their agreed terms. A slow payer can easily steal enough credit to turn a small profit into a loss. The cost of granting credit should be calculated. It includes the whole collection 'apparatus'—office, equipment, salaries for staff, stationery, postal fees, legal and agency fees for credit status checking and chasing of debts. Debts can be a costly investment. Can you afford such an investment? It may be worth forgoing credit in favour of cutting prices, an exercise that may result in improved cash flow and as much extra business as could be gained by offering credit—without the risk or the cost.

David Lee Barber, national sales manager of Credit Protection Association, offers the following story to point up the moral.

'I say to a customer: "This is the price for these goods. You pay me when you like—when will it be?" The client names a date in the future. I then come back to him and say: "Right. The goods will now cost such and such (a different, higher price)." The message is rammed home. After all, why should the supplier offer the same price to a good customer, who pays on time, compared to the slow payer who regards the supplier as an interest-free banker?'

Could you charge interest on late payments?

The EEC and USA are keener on charging interest on overdue accounts than are the British. But it is tempting to try to recoup some of the cost of past due debts, so it makes sense to weave into your terms of sale at least the option to levy interest charges, at a given rate, and if possible get these terms signed and agreed by the customer. In any case, spell them out loud and clear in all relevant communications. A risk of charging interest is that the customer who knows he must pay for the privilege of paying late will take as much credit as he needs—unless the rate you charge hurts sufficiently. Four to 6 per cent above bank rate is recommended. On the other hand, where there is temporary inability to settle, consider agreeing a fee for late payment. Then get it in writing.

Help them pay the money they owe you

There's more to getting paid than cheques through the post (there's a word or three about cheque frauds and how to beat them in Chapter 5), though post-dated cheques and certified cheques deserve a mention in this discussion of terms.

Accepting a post-dated cheque as a token of good faith as the goods go out is tempting and may be justified if you can be sure the client will be in funds at the date on the cheque. Post-dated cheques always arouse enthusiasm; they *feel* like money in the bank. But so far from being money in the bank, a bank will not even accept a post-dated cheque. It only becomes money in the bank—*your* bank—when it matures and is cleared. Never forget that.

Worry most about a post-dated cheque when it is offered for goods long since sent out. It invariably means the customer is on his last legs, financially speaking. When the cheque bounces, inevitably, he will complain of a 'mistake' at the bank, or promise to put some of his private funds in to cover it. He is buying time—at your expense.

A cheque is only as good as the financial standing of the account holder, isn't it? Wrong. It is only as good as his final intention. Many a time a cheque will be sent out with the best of intentions and then be 'stopped' because of some last-minute hitch in the company or individual's finances, or dissatisfaction with the goods.

The fact that stopping a cheque is technically criminal fraud is of academic interest. The road to court is a costly one (see Chapter 9) in time and energy, if not cash. The fact is that when you accept a cheque you don't always end up with cash in your pocket.

Not unless you demand a banker's draft, a cheque issued directly by the bank. Or the customer's cheque has been certified by his bank.

I remember vividly discovering the power of a banker's draft. I was buying a car for cash; well, not really a car, a Mini van. I was fed up with old bangers and determined to buy a new car to avoid the mechanical hang-ups and the long, cold waits for the A.A. Out in the West End with my new girlfriend, she would get progressively less amorous as the cold set in and the midnight Soho dustcarts hemmed in my poor decrepit wreck of a 'sports car'!

A Mini van was just about the cheapest new vehicle you could get and I had arranged a 5 per cent discount through a friend who worked for the garage. There was only one problem as I went to collect my ordered vehicle: the friend had since, unbeknown to me, quit working for the garage.

The manager was aghast. Five per cent! He doubted if he could run to $2\frac{1}{2}$ per cent; he never did, he said. I pulled out the banker's draft made out for 95 per cent of the list price and thrust it under his nose. 'Here it is,' I said, 'all made out.'

I drove away in my new white Mini van, happier, and also wiser, in the knowledge that a banker's draft doesn't look like cash but, by golly, it has the power of cash.

A banker's draft may not mention the customer, merely the bank concerned. A certified cheque carries a bank signature and stamp. For something that is supposed to remove all doubt about non-payment you'd think a banker's draft and certified cheque would be unmistakable, instantly recognizable. Not so. There are many types and it's worth getting your staff to pop along to your bank for a short course in species recognition.

Promissory notes

A promissory note is a bit like a post-dated cheque. It constitutes a promise to pay a certain sum on a certain date. The amount could be considerable. A promissory note can be traded with a third party, like a cheque. Promissory notes are unconditional undertakings and establish irrefutably that the buyer owes the amount stated. A collateral note is a *secured* promissory note.

Bills of exchange

A promissory note, like a cheque, is offered by the debtor to his creditor. The bill of exchange is offered by the creditor to his debtor. The latter signs and writes across it the word 'accepted.' Without this acceptance a bill of exchange is worthless.

Endorsed bills—endorsed, usually, by a financially powerful third party—are eminently negotiable and may be discounted with ease. A bill of exchange is a promise to pay on a specific date and shows the clear intention to pay and the creditor's entitlement to the sum stated. Bills of exchange are commonly used in export.

How barter could help you 'get blood from a stone'

In the bad old days when you returned dud goods to a store and asked for your money back they used to kick up a stink. You could have a replacement, or a credit note, or something different for the same price; but the last thing they would return was the cash. Now, thanks to the better-toothed consumer laws, it's easier to get back cash; but the reluctance to part with pound notes lingers.

The shop is reluctant to part with cash for two reasons. By giving back money they also abandon their profit, and a profit removed from a trading account looks (and feels) like a loss, not a sale that was never made. Also, the customer is then free to take his money elsewhere, so the competition gets a free meal. This double desire, to both retain goodwill and maintain profit, can be used to good effect if you are prepared to accept payment in kind, not cash.

In chapter 6, I tell you how to turn a bad debt into a good television set; if a trader doesn't have the readies (or won't part with money without a time-, cash- and energy-consuming fight) he may yet be willing to trade goods to clear the debt.

But how about setting up deals that never mention cash from the outset? Barter is nothing new. In North Africa camels or fine Arab steeds for wives have been commonplace transactions since the dawn of history; vegetables and eggs from the farm for beer or wine were common deals in medieval England. In the early 1800s, American Indians were happy to accept white and blue porcelain beads from Italy as payment for goods. The white man got something for next-to-nothing. But the Indian thought he was on to a good thing, too. A smart, beaded buckskin shirt was worth an awful lot of furs. And a lot of swops went on in the Second World War: sex for silk stockings, and so on...

Business by barter is carried on at the highest levels. We traded aircraft with the Finns in exchange for vodka, earth-moving equipment and liquorice. Gillette swopped blades for butter with Hungary in 1968. Because of the difficulty of getting any worthwhile currency out of the Communist bloc, pop groups set up barter deals as payment. Russia paid Boney M with furs for concert dates and Swedish group Abba receive oil and potatoes as their due for record royalties from East European states.

Barter is big business in the USA especially. Dated or hard-to-shift goods, such as cosmetics or clothes, find a market anywhere in the world where there is a worthwhile quid pro quo to be had, though cash is hard to come by. In America it's also *little* business, with what are known as 'free-sharing clubs' pooling the skills and resources of local people to create a kind of swop shop of talent.

An accountant might find himself doing the books for an interior designer who is restyling the accountant's home in return. Service swops, as opposed to an exchange of concrete goods, are easier to keep quiet about as 'gentlemen's agreements.' No records are kept, and so far the Internal Revenue Service (IRS) has turned a blind eye.

In America, one West Coast barter organization notches up notional dollar credits for services rendered. So cash credits can accumulate but, so far, they too have not attracted the attention of the IRS. Indeed, one member used his credit as security for a bank loan!

The UK has a similar operation, Business Barter, headed up by Edwin Thirlwell in Darlington. Although the deals are fully documented and therefore liable to VAT and tax assessment, there are hidden bonuses. The firms that swop goods or services at normal retail prices do more business, plus—and here's the point, as far as this book is concerned—they don't have to wait months to get paid.

In a good deal, one that doesn't involve parting with cash (blood from a stone), a firm will usually pull out all the stops to deliver its goods in double quick time. Of course the goods are worth money. But because they don't *look* like money, and because there is the element of profit, it doesn't *feel* like money. The medium is the message, to quote Marshall McLuhan out of context.

One British 'Barterbank' acts as broker for clients whose cash-per-hour earning power is used as collateral. Thus a plumber whose time might be worth £10 an hour would need to do two hours' worth of work to get 30 minutes' worth of private dentistry, because a dentist's time is worth that much more.

Private arrangements such as these, made between consenting adults in private, may well pass muster as far as the authorities (VAT and tax men) are concerned. But a business may find itself in very deep water if the value of service or goods, whether or not overtly linked to cash, is not entered in its books.

Creating a schedule of receivables

If you have the smallest of small business your accounts receivable may consist of an envelope wallet of outstanding copy invoices, statements and reminder letters. Scribbled on the letters may be a note of the outcome of a telephone conversation, perhaps with the date and a note to yourself for further action.

As your business grows, and with it your debts, so you will need to chart debts and payment progress. You will need to know, at a glance, how much of your money is tied up in dues and past dues, and how bad the latter are in terms of days outstanding. Then you can easily work out your average collection period for all the cash owing.

How efficient is your collection technique? Are you performing as well as, worse than, or better than others in your line of trade? Such questions are answerable once you've got what is known as an ageing schedule (see Figure 3.1).

How to work out your DSO—days sales outstanding

Some firms review their DSO every year. Is this often enough for you? Probably it isn't regular enough for any business. If the results aren't right, then change will be needed. Changing habits is generally slow anyway, so the quicker it's started, the better.

Let's take a three-month period: April, May, June. Work out the average amount owing at the end of those months. Then multiply by the number of days in the quarter, 90, and divide by the total credit sales made in that three-month period.

Say you were owed £1000 at end April, £1850 at end May and £1150 at end June. The average balance is £1000. Suppose that over the three months you sold goods worth £2000. Multiply £1000 by 90 and divide by £2000:

$$\frac{1000 \times 90}{2000} = 45 \text{ days}$$

Your DSO is 45 days. Forty-five days is a fairly typical collection delay in America; UK businessmen need to have another fortnight's patience, on average, or more. It depends on your trade or profession. A magazine offers to pay its writer after 90 days whether the article has been published or not. A wholesale bookseller advertised: 'We will promote to the maximum suitable titles from any publishers who give us a discount of 50 per cent and 120 days credit.' In the jewellery trade (large companies) an average collection period of 1.81 days has been recorded.... A rule of thumb guide is that the collection period should not exceed the stated terms by more than 10 or 15 days.

A few years ago Paul Williams, the controller of one of the British units of an American company known as AMAX, devised an intriguing variation on the DSO theme, a refinement of the measurement technique which may well be useful to British businessmen. The thesis was presented by Frank W. Wey, general credit manager of AMAX Inc., as an occasional paper to the Credit Research Foundation Inc. of New York. The Foundation has generously given permission for the paper to be summarized in these pages.

Overdue Accounts Control Sheet — Prepared for use in conjunction with the services of the Commercial Collection Division of Dun & Bradstreet Ltd.

Name of Account	Total Receivables	Not Due	Overdue days				Action Taken					Remarks
			Up to 30	31-60	61-90	91 +			Red Reminder	Sent to D&B	Outcome	
												0880 CCD S26

Figure 3.1 **Overdue accounts control sheet**

MEASURING THE IMPACT OF PAST-DUE ACCOUNTS ON THE RECEIVABLES PORTFOLIO

AMAX Inc. is a decentralized natural resources company with an annual sales volume over one billion dollars. A diversified company, AMAX major products include copper, lead, zinc, molybdenum, coal, potash, aluminum and iron ore. As one would expect, the industries served by AMAX and the terms granted vary widely. Both the volume and the diversity of the receivables so generated create significant problems of control.

For many years AMAX has used the three basic measures of receivable control monitored by the Credit Research Foundation, namely, days sales outstanding in receivables (or DSO), the percentage of receivables current and the percentage of receivables over 90 days past due. By far the most important measure has been DSO. DSO measures money tied up in days, but it makes no distinction between terms and delinquency. As such it is a good measure of management performance, but a poor measure of credit department performance.

DSO does offer important benefits. It enables us to compare ourselves to our industry and to ourselves in prior periods. Sometimes however it is incorrectly used to compare dissimilar units within our own company. In addition, some managers tend to equate DSO with credit-department performance. This tendency is not hard to understand, since the impact of management decisions regarding terms has never been adequately explained. In sum, DSO has been a good tool when properly understood to be a symptom and not a root cause.

The percentage of receivables current and the percentage of receivables over 90 days past due have also been imperfect devices for measuring receivables. Sharp sales fluctuations cause large movements in both percentages, thus beclouding rather than enlightening the situation. Careful analysis will always uncover these anomalies, but given the time pressures under which managers work, cursory inspection is much more likely than careful analysis.

The heart of the receivable-measurement problem then has been imperfect tools inadequately understood.

We now have a device for measuring receivables that seems to overcome most of the shortcomings of the usual measures. It was *not* the result of painstaking analysis. It was developed through the insight of Paul Williams, the controller of one of AMAX British units.

Since we knew of no DSO statistics by which a British company could compare itself to its industry, we suggested that they should compare their actual DSO to their best possible DSO. Paul Williams responded by suggesting that we could calculate best possible DSO by using the standard Credit Research Foundation (CRF) formula but substituting current receivables for total receivables in the formula. From that suggestion we have developed two new measurement tools.

The CRF formula for DSO is:

$$\frac{\text{Average receivables for 3 month-ends} \times 90}{\text{3 month sales}} = \text{DSO}$$

The Williams formula for best possible DSO is:

$$\frac{\text{Average } \textit{current} \text{ receivables for 3 month-ends} \times 90}{\text{3 month sales}} = \text{BP DSO}$$

If we think about the latter formula, we realize that if all our customers paid us exactly on the due date, all receivables would be in the current aging column. Hence, if we use the current receivables figure in the CRF formula for DSO we will get best possible DSO or *average terms.*

To carry our reasoning one step further, if we subtract Average Terms from DSO we have *average cost of delinquency* in days (or ACD).

What we have done in fact is to break up DSO into its two components, Average Terms and ACD. Now we can spell out to management the impact of their terms decisions with Average Terms. Since Average Terms, by definition, takes into account only the current receivables, the measure isolates the actual selling terms on which the calculation is based. Further it permits an examination of those terms, to see if they are reasonable within the industry and justifiable in terms of the seller's production time, ability to carry receivables, and alternative corporate uses to which those funds may be put.

Once the reasonableness of Average Terms has been established, the technique may next be used to measure credit-department operations via ACD. Marketing objectives and cost of capital considerations may be weighed against each other to determine an optimum goal for ACD; variations from this optimum ACD may then be examined for their effects on profits and financial costs. It is possible, for example, that management may wish to maintain an ACD of between 15 and 17 days, because this level of ACD may enable the company to keep a significant larger share of the market than would, say, a 10-day ACD; the additional profits from sales at the 15 - 17 day ACD would more than offset the additional cost of carrying delinquent receivables the extra 5 - 7 days.

We can now also calculate the average cost of delinquency in money terms by multiplying ACD times average daily sales. Thus we can quantify the real meaning of ACD.

Let's work some numbers through the formulas outlined above:

Month	Sales (£'000)	Total receivables (£'000)	Current receivables (£'000)
July	9324	14935	9519
August	10960	17078	11713
September	9371	15936	9459
	29655	47949	30691

$$\text{DSO} = \frac{(47\,949 \div 3) \times 90}{29655} = 48.5 \text{ days}$$

$$\text{Average Terms} = \frac{(30\,691 \div 3) \times 90}{29655} = 31.0 \text{ days}$$

$$\text{ACD} = 48.5 - 31.0 = 17.5 \text{ days}$$

Thus we find that the average terms for this unit are 31.0 days and the average cost of delinquency is 17.5 days.

To quantify ACD we multiply average daily sales times ACD:

$$(29\,655 \div 90) \times 17.5 = 5766$$

Thus we learn that this unit has £5766000 additional average investment in receivables caused by delinquency.

Earlier in this monograph we indicated that these new tools seem to overcome most of the shortcomings of the old measures. They do not overcome all the shortcomings. Wide swings in sales will affect Average Terms and ACD just as they now affect DSO and the percentages current and over 90 days past due. However, that difficulty may be overcome by making the same calculations on a 12-month moving average, i.e., substituting 12 for 3, and 360 for 90, in the basic formulas.

The major advantages of these new measurements:

1. They are simple to use.
2. They are easy to understand.
3. They distinguish between terms and delinquency.
4. They enable us to quantify the average cost of delinquency.
5. We already have the data.

4. How to sense trouble

The best time to sense trouble is before you get involved. The next best time is after you have been doing business with the bounder, but well before you get caught for cash. The last thing you want to develop is trouble-shooting hindsight.

Rat smelling is possible at many levels. We all do it, every day. Sussing new people out is normal. It's natural to measure a man up when you first meet him, no malice intended. Nor do you need special detective skills; everyday signs are your first clues. Cleanliness and smartness of appearance is taken for granted in business. But good clothes cost money; styles change and what was 'in' a couple of years ago may look decidedly démodé today (think how uncouth flared trousers and wide lapels look now); and cleaning bills are big ones, too.

One of the most expensive items of male clothing are shoes. It's tempting to skimp on one or more aspects of clothing. To wear good but dated suits, new but not so clean outfits, and scuffed shoes or shoes with composite, not leather, soles—because who is likely to look that far down?

It remains a curious fact of life that people rarely cheat about their appearance. A man will dress to precisely the level that his income allows. The car he drives will exactly correspond to his niche in life. Drivers of company cars are neatly categorized according to the vehicles they drive. The rep has his Cortina, a middle manager his Granada, and a director aspires to a Rover. If the marques change from company to company, the relative cost/status of the cars remain remarkably constant through a variety of dissimilar businesses. I know a man who runs a successful country bakery and runs around in a white Rover to impress his customers. It does, but he can afford it! Rogues apart, why people rarely fake their status by enhancing their image out of all proportion to their income or position remains a mystery.

The result is that a man's clothes, shoes, brief-case, personal hygiene are all pointers to the sort of treatment you are likely to get when it comes to paying *your* bill. If he can't pay his own clothing bills, is it likely he will pay yours? If a new prospect hedges with the ticket in a restaurant as you meet for the first time, if he sidesteps his round in the pub, how will he react when your chunky invoices land on his desk?

So you can, as it were, rely on the 'honesty'—or at least lack of guile—of many folk to help you assess their personal spending power. But independent businessmen have more to spend than their own money. They have their company's money. How they dispose of it speaks volumes. That's why it will pay you to visit the working location of your intending debtor. Even before you enter there's a lot of potentially valuable information to be gleaned—just use your eyes.

If his turnover goes down, will he turn *you* over?

If this is a retail premises, is it in a good trading area? One of the classic mistakes a new trader makes is opting for cheaper rent, away from the busiest part of town. Pretty soon he discovers his false economy: he's paying a cut price to be where the business isn't!

But busy shopping centres can decline, too. Is this one on the up? Or are there too many shops clad in estate agents' signs? Shops that carry no goods, like a betting shop or building society office, are also poor companions to the retail trade. Are there charity shops, such as Oxfam and Save the Children around? Could it be the landlord charges a 'charitable' rent because he can get no better? Is this a market street—in which case it may be busy only on one or two days a week? Nothing is more revealing (if you or an assistant has the time) than to stand outside an establishment, at peak shopping times, and monitor who goes in, what calibre of customer, how many buy, and suchlike.

Did you have an easy time in getting to the store by car—and getting out? Is it well served by public transport and landscaped with free car parts; or is it tucked into a medieval side street, festooned with double yellow no-parking lines and thickly forested with parking meters? Your prospective client may have spoken big about expansion plans. But has he got room to grow in his present situation?

Inside, is the reception comfortable, pleasantly decorated; are you made to feel at ease, are your particulars pleasantly and efficiently taken? When a business is on the way down in the retail trade the shelves start to empty, because the shopkeeper is winding up and/or cannot get supplies because he has lost his credit standing and has no cash. Surfaces also gather dust when business dries up, and a generally run-down office is also a bad sign.

A neglected or unsanitary loo is a very poor omen. Leadership is from the top; but the bottom counts, too! Worse still, is where there is a plush directors' privy but a graffiti-daubed cesspit for the workers. 'What about the workers?' is a question the prospective creditor should always ask. 'Them and us' attitudes, exemplified in the language of the boss and executed in the layout of the business, bode ill. Lack of creature comforts—heat, light, good ventilation—can lead to absenteeism and even strike action; modernization of a hopelessly out-of-date factory will prove costly and time-consuming.

Flashy, expensive cars in the directors' compound are not necessarily a sign of thriving business; they may merely indicate that the big boys cream off their unjust deserts instead of ploughing profits back into equipment and raw materials. Serious business people also are suspicious of another status symbol: decorative dolly birds. The assumption, unreasoned but almost universal, is that (a) they are inefficient workers and/or (b) they are for the directors' out-of-hours' titillation...

Look, too, for evidence of good organization, smooth production, without obvious hiccups in the shape of ancient shipping orders, cancelled or returned, lying about the yard. The one time when chaos can be condoned is when a new company is obviously rushed off its feet with fresh business and has not got the time to clear up the mess. But here the telltale signs are different—the latest machinery and office gadgets peeking out of their partly-opened wrappings; supersmart coffee and water machines in every corridor, instead of the washed-out-looking cleaning lady trundling her tea urn; a new typewriter on every secretary's new desk; evidence that executives use time cost-effectively, evidenced by personal dictate-as-you-walk tape recorders; and so on.

The references you want are the ones they don't give

If the firm produces goods that need to be transported from their yard do they have their own transport? Is it modern, in good condition? If customers send their own vehicles to collect, you collect the customers' names from the painted logo on the side. Then, when you come to garner references, if these names don't feature you'll know who to approach in addition. New clients notoriously offer trade references they *know* will give them a good write-up. Such references may well have been cultivated especially for the purpose—to the detriment of others who are kept waiting for payment. It's the *others* you want to talk to!

The point was succinctly put by a London commercial investigator: 'If you see a man who gives Wrangler jeans as a reference, but you notice that he stocks both Wrangler and Levis, approach Levis and find out how he pays them.' Not only are the British notoriously shy about asking for money owed to them, they are also slow in coming forward when it's money *information* they want. You can get a surprising amount of information out of companies merely by asking for it, according to this investigator. 'You just phone them up, as a potential granter of credit to XYZ company, and ask: "Have you had any problems with XYZ?" Have you had any cheques returned is what you're trying to find out. It's amazing how many companies come up with information.'

How to stop worrying about credit and get on with the serious business of doing business

Of course there isn't always time to see people to discuss their credit rating. Or distance is the problem. Yet you must have some indication of a new customer's credit standing—or must you? The credit executive of one of our biggest paper companies is seriously considering scrapping credit tests below a certain amount. According to the commercial accountant at one of our leading paper producers and processors, in line with the Pareto Principle* (80 per cent of a company's business is done with 20 per cent of its customers), it is to the vital 20 per cent that the big guns should be turned.

'Eighty-five per cent of our customers pull in only about 15 per cent of our business' (the Pareto corollary). In fact, he is beginning to question the value of routine dunning letters: 'We are good payers ourselves—by the 10th of the month following date of invoice—yet we receive umpteen dunning letters every month!'

In his experience, letters have no effect on the majority of small customers: they pay in six weeks anyway. 'My inclination is to let a bill go to £500 and then to send one letter stating: "You have exceeded your terms and we will not only sue you but we will also close your account".'

The rationale behind this novel strategy is as follows. His firm gets about 350 requests a month to open accounts. It takes time and money to vet them all, to sift through a salesmen's reports and take up two trade and bank references. With the cost of sending any original (not form or stereotype letter) at around a fiver (I have heard it put at £9, taking into account secretarial and executive time, rental of premises, office equipment, postal clerks' time, stationery, and so on) he says the exercise is ridiculously costly. For each of 300-odd people, 900 letters, plus a stamped s.a.e.; given a gross margin of profit, in his business, of only 10 per cent, doing away with credit checks could be a valuable cost-cutting exercise. The hope and expectation is, of course, that once it becomes known that they are prepared to give instant, no-questions-asked credit, they will pick up even more business than at present. Only if a customer says that the £500 trading limit is not enough will they take up trade references.

But there is a danger. What happens when the minnow turns into a mackerel,

* Vilfredo Pareto.

when the company that operated happily under a £500 ceiling finds the ceiling too low? To qualify for more substantial credit, it will have to submit to the usual vetting, restrictions and tightly controlled terms. The commercial accountant's inclination is to suck that one and see, to try it on a section of the trade and take if from there.

It's worth taking time to find out what they're worth

More often you will want, however, not to trust to luck, judgement, or the little-known laws of self-regulation. Instead, you will attempt to assess the credit rating of people to whom you are about to grant credit. Is there a cheap, simple and relatively painless method that has proved its effectiveness in the market place?

Mr J. S. Martin, managing director of Brent (Hailsham) Ltd of Sussex, has forthright views on all aspects of credit control. He sends round a rep to check, among other things, on the state of the business, the stock position ('A lot of fresh stock is usually a good sign'), and, important where the competition is close by, whether this new customer is likely to usurp the trade of other established customers—Brent are mainly wholesalers and manufacturers of fishing tackle.

The prospect is then asked to complete an Application for Credit Account form (see Figure 4.1). There is the usual request for a bank and two trade references (which must not be associated companies) and a request for a letterhead. Most important, says Mr Martin, because this will usually show the correct name and address, correct trading style or title of the company, VAT number, registered number and registered address of the company, and possibly also the directors' names. 'You'd be surprised how many reps get the details wrong,' says Mr Martin. They're apparently too busy chatting and selling. Yet if the crunch comes, and a debt goes bad and comes before the courts, your suit may well foul up simply because you have used the wrong name.

Letters requesting references (see below) should be brief, factual and *confidential*:

PRIVATE AND CONFIDENTIAL

Dear Sir

N. Air Doogood & Sons Ltd

The above named firm has given your company as a trade reference. Will you help us by answering the questions over the page? Please return this letter in the stamped envelope provided.

Your comments will be held in strict confidence.

Manufacturers & Wholesale Distributors of FISHING TACKLE AND ELECTRICAL EQUIPMENT

Brent (Hailsham) Ltd.

Directors J S Martin *(Managing)* J F Martin
Secretary F L Warnes

Registered Office
STATION ROAD, HAILSHAM, EAST SUSSEX, BN27 2SA Telephone Hailsham 840094 Telegrams Brent Ltd. Hailsham
Registered in England No. 568303 VAT Registration No. 190 1974 53

APPLICATION FOR CREDIT ACCOUNT

NAME OF COMPANY: ....

ADDRESS: ....
....
....
....

TELEPHONE NO: ....

DIRECTOR/OWNER/
PARTNER(S) ....

HALF DAY CLOSING: ....

BANKERS: ....
....
....
....

* 1st TRADE REF: ....
....
....

* 2nd TRADE REF: ....
....
....

* N.B. Not Associated Companies.

FOR RECORD PURPOSES A COPY OF LETTERHEAD WOULD BE APPRECIATED

Figure 4.1 Application for credit account

Thank you for your time and trouble. Any time we can help you in a similar situation we shall be happy to do so.

Yours faithfully

F. Ingersburn
Credit Controller

Try to name the right person, it saves time and encourages a swifter response. When in doubt, write to the managing director. It is a curious fact of business life that people like to talk to their counterparts in business. It confirms the justness of the system, avoids making a man feel he is being talked down to. So if you are writing to a credit controller, and you are a two-partner concern in which your wife acts as secretary, company secretary and dunning-letter writer, call her a Credit Controller, too—and get a better response.

One-sheet letters are preferable; there is less bumpf for the recipient to handle. If he wants to take a photocopy, he can. On the other hand, if he sends it back it is truly confidential as far as he is concerned for there is no record in *his* company's files!

The information requested is as follows:

How long have you known...?
How do you regard them?
What terms do you offer them?
What is their highest ever credit rating with you?
Do they pay well, slow, average?
What is their highest recent payment?

You must expect to be given the names only of favourable referees. Your new client will also have contacted them to expect the reference request, as is normal, polite business practice. He may have gone further and 'organized' a glowing testimonial. You cannot protect against this, but there are signs that should set the warning bells jangling.

Most people do not know how to lie convincingly. They ham it up, speak only praises, and leave out the mote of the mixed blessing that is the sure sign of a genuine character reference. If the two references are similarly phrased this may mean the prospect has written them both and got friends to sign them.

Is there a hint that the reference is not from a long-established, respected trader but a fiver-a-week accommodation address? You may need to check out the creditworthiness of the reference—not so easy if the company isn't limited. And you may have no protection where the reference is good but the facts wrong—because the target company has been taken over by a villain (your prospective customer), but the referee doesn't know it.

You may need independent information, and need to go to a credit-reference agency, of which more later. A bank reference or 'banker's opinion' will also be wanted. You will have to work through your own bank, as that is the way banks prefer to operate:

PRIVATE AND CONFIDENTIAL

The Manager
My Bank Ltd
78 High Street
Anytown

Dear Sir

N. Air Doogood & Sons Ltd

Your help in our enquiries concerning the above named will be greatly appreciated.

Will you therefore ask of ...... bank whether their client can be considered good for £ ...... credit on 30-day bills.

Yours faithfully

is a typical request.

The bank reference or 'banker's opinion' is vulnerable to fixing. Just as it is known for traders to cultivate suppliers by keeping to a fault-free payment routine, so they will keep the manager of a particular bank branch sweet by never dipping into the red. Even a bank manager with a dodgy customer will try to keep a poker face and a semblance of confidentiality and impartiality. So you'll need to read between his lines when the verdict appears.

'Good for your figure' is good enough. 'Considered good for your figure' is not quite so sure. 'We cannot speak for your figure' is bad news. The best report is also the briefest: 'Undoubted.' And when you're contacting the bank it's as well to check that the company hasn't recently changed hands and is now being run by rogues: 'Is... well established under its present management?' is the usual prompt.

Is XYZ company a good credit bet?

Never take a company at face value. An established company on the slide normally goes down slowly, but not always: remember Rolls-Royce? Sound credit assessment demands a good long look at basics, like the names and backgrounds of the partners or directors, views of main suppliers and their bank, the amount of capital employed, financial structure, how long the firm has been in business, copy of the balance sheet, proper trading style (name), exact address and also registered address (if different).

Watch out if a director has been associated with a previous failed venture.

Take care where there is a sign of excessive directors' loans to the company, though family business is traditionally financed in this way in Britain. But where the loan is secured by a debenture, beware. When a company goes to the wall, debenture holders come first in the share-out, then other secured creditors and last of all those whose debts are unsecured.

If trade reports come through with tales of woe and stories of ever-lengthening gaps between payments, liberties taken with discount, sudden returns of goods purchased, then the writing may well be on the wall. Regular, sluggish payment is not untypical (it may even be acceptable) and at least the pattern is predictable. Change is usually the precursor of demise, with a new picture emerging of erratically late payments, excuses, part-payment and the whole gamut of 'stall stories' well known to the seasoned credit watcher.

Clues for the amateur credit sleuth

Before ever you enter these troubled waters you will want to look under the bed of the company you are about to keep. How is the firm with which you are considering trading made up? Analysis of balance sheets is a major study and outside the scope of this book. But credit clues are thick on the ground even for the amateur credit sleuth.

The economic climate has a marked effect on the credit performance of traders. But if a company can't manage itself through a recession, what will happen if there's a sudden downturn? Indeed, this is rather more likely than the reverse; a boom is usually the reward of plodding effort, inspired selling strategy, rather than any freak upturn in market conditions.

What you really want to know is how liquid is the company under the microscope? How much cash does it have? How much of its assets could be quickly turned into cash in time of crisis?

Current liabilities (creditors, tax, dividends, overdraft, etc.) are divided into current assets (debtors, cash) but minus the stock:

$$\frac{\text{Liquid assets}}{\text{Current liabilities}} = \text{the liquid ratio}$$

The liquid ratio is also known as the 'acid test.'

The liquid ratio can be too good. If a company is well established and trading well, perhaps it would be wiser to put more back into the business, to finance more stocks. Other useful figures include debt as a percentage of shareholders' funds, the *gearing ratio*. High-debt industries, like hotels, shipping, house builders, often score 160 per cent. If a secure company has little debt, this, too, may be a fault. Borrowed capital could be used to finance expansion. On the other hand, companies that rely heavily on outside borrowing, or that show a steadily declining net profit figure, may not be able to ride out a recession.

Firms that traditionally better the 1:1 mark for their liquid ratio are office equipment, mail order, the metal industry, chemicals. Industries revealing less than a ratio of 0:6 are hotels, house-builders, hotel and food retailers.

The slightly less urgent integer of a company's solvency is the Current Ratio:

$$\text{Current ratio} = \frac{\text{current assets}}{\text{current liabilities}}$$

This shows the amount of working capital. Technically, the firm has gone bust when its liabilities are greater than its assets. The value of the stocks is not included in the liquid ratio for a variety of reasons. For one, bankrupt stock sells badly, or the stock may be incomplete in the sense that it is unfinished, needing to be passed to another company for a further process. Some stocks, such as those of the clothing trade, are notoriously valueless once the season or fashion fad has passed.

The two main debt ratios are:

$$\text{Bad debt ratio} = \frac{\text{Bad debts} \times 100}{\text{Credit sales}}$$

giving the percentage of bad debts to credit sales (total sales figure is sometimes given), and:

$$\text{Collection period} = \frac{\text{annual net sales on credit terms}}{365}$$

This gives the average daily credit sales into notes and accounts receivable, including any discounted. A concern making annual sales of £365000 on open account terms has an average daily credit sale of £1000. If the total notes and accounts receivable of the firm stand at £32000 the collection period is 32 days.

If a company is letting its debtors get away with murder, you may figure it will let you do the same. Or you may conclude it's badly run and should be avoided (try the collection-period ratio on your own figures), as it will soon go bust.

But how slow is a slow payer? A quick glance at the Dun & Bradstreet Accounts Receivable Control Calendar is revealing (see Figure 4.2). It shows the collection periods for 22 business sectors.

A large instrument engineering firm typically waits 72.05 days to get paid; a small footwear retailer is kept waiting 3.61 days; a medium size food and drink wholesaler is 24.48 days unpaid. The range is astonishing, and all of it is 'normal' for these trades!

MANUFACTURING

		Large Companies A	Large Companies B	Large Companies C	Medium Companies A	Medium Companies B	Medium Companies C	Small Companies A	Small Companies B	Small Companies C	Total Manufacturers A	Total Manufacturers B	Total Manufacturers C
1	TEXTILES (EXCL. CARPETS)	59.67	51.62	37.87	62.30	55.37	37.49	64.80	50.23	34.97	61.94	53.27	37.87
2	CARPETS	61.32	58.21	40.16	62.34	51.75	33.82	62.52	54.81	38.83	61.32	52.79	39.01
3	CLOTHING	50.34	38.06	17.49	66.08	48.84	27.46	55.37	47.85	31.21	57.77	43.91	24.84
4	FOOTWEAR	33.76	28.75	24.86	45.99	26.55	15.36	34.30	29.63	22.29	36.64	28.75	21.26
5	LEATHER & FURS	—	—	—	56.48	46.03	27.40	51.28	37.69	22.05	53.48	39.12	26.52
6	FOOD & DRINK	34.13	24.07	12.77	50.89	33.03	19.53	38.29	26.78	18.96	40.67	28.21	18.28
7	CHEMICALS	73.80	62.40	49.48	78.47	67.40	58.53	77.65	64.44	45.09	77.05	64.40	54.54
8	TIMBER & FURNITURE	73.34	54.76	44.11	74.74	57.66	43.01	81.63	54.32	44.35	73.34	55.55	44.10
9	PAPER	71.72	59.26	48.73	77.65	66.14	54.96	78.82	62.22	40.77	74.25	62.67	49.07
10	PRINTING & PUBLISHING	78.25	64.95	48.33	82.10	64.36	37.89	100.47	63.76	43.32	82.10	64.36	43.32
11	BRICKS, POTTERY & GLASS	73.10	66.15	42.63	72.73	56.03	48.07	72.84	57.66	42.36	72.76	58.89	44.62
12	JEWELLERY & PRECIOUS METALS	—	—	—	78.61	57.94	49.17	78.72	60.14	46.62	74.11	57.94	46.97
13	METALS (NON PRECIOUS)	70.96	58.33	38.24	86.19	72.36	45.21	86.12	73.99	58.59	76.77	64.99	46.66
14	METAL GOODS	77.01	68.42	59.15	90.25	77.05	48.74	84.16	76.04	56.89	83.55	72.16	56.42
15	MECHANICAL ENGINEERING	79.50	66.58	41.71	91.79	67.27	48.82	84.19	75.68	60.95	83.40	70.38	51.57
16	INSTRUMENT ENGINEERING	82.99	72.05	56.51	91.12	70.97	61.36	87.95	65.40	49.49	85.81	70.94	57.97
17	ELECTRICAL ENGINEERING	79.04	68.00	45.46	82.14	71.39	53.47	93.31	79.24	58.83	82.28	71.45	53.47
18	GARAGE & MOTOR REPAIRS (DISTRIBUTING AND SERVICING)	21.02	15.27	12.20	20.60	14.10	8.74	15.69	11.08	7.58	19.65	14.03	9.40
19	CONSTRUCTION (CIVIL ENGINEERING AND PUBLIC WORKS)	54.69	18.35	9.15	73.95	52.79	34.81	87.92	58.10	36.03	67.49	48.52	18.35
20	HAULAGE (SERVICES)	79.75	72.31	55.97	81.49	70.28	56.77	85.39	78.89	65.37	82.48	72.92	60.72
21	HOTELS RESTAURANTS & CATERING (SERVICES)	35.37	27.89	12.66	39.66	22.88	11.38	33.38	18.95	6.48	35.37	21.89	11.38
22	ADVERTISING (SERVICES)	61.33	47.25	41.12	72.85	58.64	46.76	73.24	62.36	48.91	70.45	55.21	43.82

WHOLESALING

		Large Companies A	Large Companies B	Large Companies C	Medium Companies A	Medium Companies B	Medium Companies C	Small Companies A	Small Companies B	Small Companies C	Total Wholesalers A	Total Wholesalers B	Total Wholesalers C
1	TEXTILES (EXCL. CARPETS)	52.77	37.86	25.83	61.38	43.97	31.05	71.42	53.90	35.73	61.38	44.68	31.05
2	CARPETS	—	—	—	62.80	45.54	25.88	57.52	48.39	20.10	57.56	47.28	25.88
3	CLOTHING	—	—	—	64.24	51.01	31.40	67.01	52.05	33.76	64.24	52.05	33.11
4	FOOTWEAR	—	—	—	42.34	34.64	21.31	43.45	33.36	22.92	43.45	33.36	22.22
5	LEATHER & FURS	50.10	40.45	29.56	57.12	43.99	20.67	65.66	41.04	14.14	57.12	40.45	23.76
6	FOOD & DRINK	28.97	16.36	12.26	30.58	24.48	16.07	57.73	35.93	12.42	35.93	22.23	13.35
7	CHEMICALS	67.99	52.09	44.32	65.23	60.40	39.63	61.77	49.91	30.77	65.23	53.27	34.95
8	TIMBER & FURNITURE	76.65	62.42	55.64	76.96	65.35	53.79	67.32	59.62	50.12	73.51	62.42	52.20
9	PAPER	76.06	72.51	53.19	80.43	73.58	58.39	78.97	65.93	46.26	79.18	70.72	53.01
10	PRINTING & PUBLISHING	—	—	—	53.67	29.46	21.62	69.76	42.79	26.61	59.22	32.43	24.73
11	BRICKS, POTTERY & GLASS	60.65	55.50	41.60	71.68	60.84	54.16	63.32	50.28	42.00	63.09	55.54	45.12
12	JEWELLERY & PRECIOUS METALS	46.90	8.99	1.18	64.91	46.34	26.65	77.73	51.82	14.92	68.21	45.73	8.99
13	METALS (NON PRECIOUS) (DISTRIBUTING)	74.10	53.57	17.61	84.52	70.75	39.14	78.48	68.46	41.35	77.84	63.26	37.13
14	METAL GOODS	—	—	—	81.28	71.90	58.77	83.08	70.25	56.78	81.28	69.38	57.38
15	MECHANICAL ENGINEERING (DISTRIBUTING)	96.51	51.86	33.49	91.12	63.26	52.23	87.86	77.22	56.31	91.12	65.67	45.07
16	INSTRUMENT ENGINEERING	76.65	60.15	31.14	74.63	53.24	35.89	83.83	50.77	30.06	76.65	53.80	31.14
17	ELECTRICAL ENGINEERING	70.58	63.93	49.90	77.85	69.93	53.73	81.84	70.51	46.03	75.87	66.71	49.91
18	GARAGE & MOTOR REPAIRS	—	—	—	—	—	—	—	—	—	—	—	—
19	CONSTRUCTION (GENERAL BUILDING)	36.78	15.96	8.88	51.56	21.53	10.35	62.38	31.63	14.97	45.58	21.23	10.35
20	HAULAGE	—	—	—	—	—	—	—	—	—	—	—	—
21	HOTELS RESTAURANTS & CATERING	—	—	—	—	—	—	—	—	—	—	—	—
22	ADVERTISING	—	—	—	—	—	—	—	—	—	—	—	—

RETAILING

		Large Companies A	Large Companies B	Large Companies C	Medium Companies A	Medium Companies B	Medium Companies C	Small Companies A	Small Companies B	Small Companies C	Total Retailers A	Total Retailers B	Total Retailers C
1	TEXTILES (EXCL. CARPETS)	—	—	—	16.33	9.70	3.40	34.82	11.08	6.81	23.12	11.08	5.38
2	CARPETS	—	—	—	—	—	—	42.24	24.64	13.89	42.24	24.64	13.89
3	CLOTHING	39.56	16.27	5.95	33.58	17.74	9.16	25.77	13.08	6.73	29.19	15.10	6.92
4	FOOTWEAR	14.00	6.88	5.21	15.55	11.90	6.35	8.57	3.61	2.22	11.90	6.35	3.47
5	LEATHER & FURS	—	—	—	—	—	—	12.81	6.81	5.86	12.81	6.81	5.86
6	FOOD & DRINK	4.51	2.77	1.04	8.88	3.09	1.23	13.37	2.19	1.06	7.53	2.93	1.20
7	CHEMICALS	—	—	—	37.70	32.85	5.54	44.78	29.95	20.87	38.30	29.95	16.90
8	TIMBER & FURNITURE	106.27	33.24	11.23	54.44	39.33	11.19	43.00	23.40	11.17	52.88	28.04	11.19
9	PAPER	—	—	—	—	—	—	54.60	11.07	5.47	54.60	11.07	5.47
10	PRINTING & PUBLISHING	21.08	5.51	3.50	23.69	20.50	2.78	44.78	25.74	7.90	36.30	13.95	5.13
11	BRICKS, POTTERY & GLASS	—	—	—	—	—	—	18.15	5.24	1.87	32.31	7.01	1.87
12	JEWELLERY & PRECIOUS METALS	—	—	—	37.36	11.95	8.97	17.60	8.51	5.20	17.89	11.42	7.47
13	METALS (NON PRECIOUS)	—	—	—	—	—	—	—	—	—	—	—	—
14	METAL GOODS	—	—	—	—	—	—	53.53	32.56	10.58	53.49	34.78	11.05
15	MECHANICAL ENGINEERING	—	—	—	—	—	—	—	—	—	—	—	—
16	INSTRUMENT ENGINEERING	—	—	—	—	—	—	—	—	—	—	—	—
17	ELECTRICAL ENGINEERING	29.82	9.95	4.00	30.52	8.87	3.94	35.21	16.48	6.36	30.52	12.97	3.96
18	GARAGE & MOTOR REPAIRS	—	—	—	—	—	—	—	—	—	—	—	—
19	CONSTRUCTION (ANCILLIARY SERVICES (PAINTING — FLOORING — ROOFING ETC.)	98.47	75.61	39.99	71.73	32.09	13.72	70.19	48.47	35.07	75.61	50.60	25.99
20	HAULAGE	—	—	—	—	—	—	—	—	—	—	—	—
21	HOTELS RESTAURANTS & CATERING	—	—	—	—	—	—	—	—	—	—	—	—
22	ADVERTISING	—	—	—	—	—	—	—	—	—	—	—	—

A: UPPER QUARTILE B: MEDIAN C: LOWER QUARTILE

The Median (B) is the mid-point figure and this is the typical ratio or norm for all companies in its sub category. The Ratio half way between the Median and the top of the series is the Upper Quartile (A); the ratio at mid-point between the Median and the bottom of the range is the Lower Quartile (C). The Upper and Lower Quartiles typify the performance of companies in the top half and bottom half of the sample, respectively.

Note: These ratios are for the calendar year 1977. Ratios for 1978 and 1979 will be available shortly, see overleaf for details.†

Figure 4.2 Reproduced from a Dun & Bradstreet Ltd, Commercial Collection Division, Accounts Receivable Control Calendar. Collection periods for 22 Business Sectors

5. How to avoid trouble

In order to avoid trouble with debts it helps to know why you've got trouble in the first place. Why do business people make you wait to get paid?

A private investigator hit the nail on the head when he said that business people pay their bills either (a) when they're ready to pay or (b) when they feel they must pay.

Think about it. How often have you felt, when dealing with a debtor: 'Here, hold on a minute, it's *my* money we're talking about. . . . '? It helps the debtor to make you feel he's doing you a favour paying up at all, because then you'll be grateful for what you get whenever you get it.

Everyone is out for number one. Only the unwritten 'laws' of business stop us tearing each other's throats out. So write a few new rules—and get the jungle swinging in your direction.

Every business book and businessman will tell you that market forces dictate the sort of treatment you get in the market place. If a customer can go to any Tom, Dick or Harriet for goods similar to those you offer, at comparable prices, he will walk all over you. That's why firms knock themselves out to create in their products a USP—Unique Selling Proposition. Customers beat a path to the door of the man with an exclusive product and he can name his price (and terms) when they get there.

In a similar situation are the nationalized industries in a monopoly position. You can't travel by rail in the UK other than by British Rail; their prices, like them or not, are the ones you have to pay. Firms in a monopoly or near-monopoly niche are similarly cock-a-hoop. Oxygen and fuel suppliers have their customers over a barrel, and they tighten the screws accordingly. A typical payment plan in the petrol industry is for the tanker driver to demand a cheque for the last load before a drop of his fresh load goes into the pumps.

But what of a chap who's selling common or garden garden chairs or run-of-the-mill pepper? How can he even contemplate being worthy of preferential treatment? Likely as not, he doesn't. Instead he'll expect to be paid on time by a few duffers, kept waiting for a while by the majority, and be run ragged by a few. It's normal; it's expected; but that doesn't mean *you* have to put up with it.

Consider this parable. You, a 5ft 6in runt who gave up on his Bullworker after three days, are walking down an alleyway just wide enough to allow two people to pass side by side. Coming towards you is a man built like a tank, a face like a beat-up bouncer. He's in your 'stream'. Who changes lane, you or he? You do. Now try this one. Same situation, only the chap coming towards you is 4ft nothing. But he's wearing a karate outfit tied with a black belt. Who steps aside, you or he? You do. What for, dummy? He's no martial arts expert. He couldn't even lift the Bullworker out of its box. But he does know how to get respect!

That stunted pygmy understands the power of having the right *posture*. His impressive *image* made you think twice and shy away. It's possible to develop a powerful image in business, too. All you have to do is show, from step one, that when it comes to getting *your* bills paid you mean business.

A difficult task? Not at all. Easier done than said with the special stickers available, as of right, to members of The Credit Protection Association (see Figure 5.1). The stickers, in stark black on white, say simply:

WE ARE MEMBERS OF
The Credit Protection Association Ltd
PLEASE OBSERVE OUR CREDIT TERMS

Alongside is a drawing of a rather beady looking eye. The message, clear for all to see, is: 'We are watching you.' But there is a more subtle implication in the gentle reminder; for the suggestion is that CPA is also a credit-reporting agency. The paranoid may conclude that delinquent debtors will get their particulars taken down and may find it harder to get credit in future.

Figure 5.1 The Credit Protection Association's stickers

Hit a man in his reputation and you could be on to a good thing. The bard had it right:

The purest treasure mortal times afford
Is spotless reputation; that away,
Men are but gilded loam or painted clay. (*Richard II*, Act 1 Scene 1)

Reminder stickers are nothing new. Garishly coloured, they bear pithy messages (Figures 5.2 and 5.3). A neat statement of terms is also possible on a sticker (see Figure 5.4).

The advantage of stickers is that they save time—typing and 'thinking up'

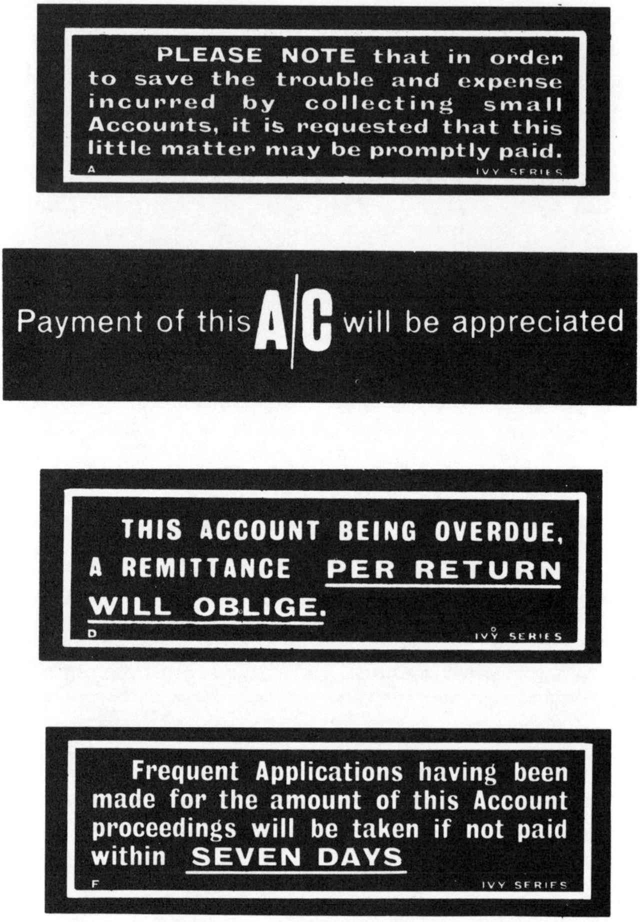

Figure 5.2 Reminder stickers

time. Often stickers make a stab at humour that, some say, ill fits the circumstances. One such, in lemon yellow with red and black printing, shows a couple of cartoon caricature businessmen, beaming and with their arms round each other. The rubric (see Figure 5.3) reads:

> friendly. . REMINDER
> Whilst friendship is essential to
> the success of our business,
> financial support is an absolute
> necessity. May we enjoy both?

Long may *you* enjoy both. But at a pinch, take the money.

Figure 5.3 Reminder stickers

TERMS: 4% 7 DAYS
2% 30 DAYS
CARRIAGE PAID OVER £75.00
ALL PAYMENTS TO BE
MADE TO THE COMPANY

Figure 5.4 Terms sticker

If you are a member of a trade protection association—and they are growing in number as the recession bites—then say so. Not only on a sticker that attaches to your invoice, but printed on to your statements, reminder letters *and* invoices.

One of the chief complaints about the sticker system is that they aren't seen by the right people, usually only a lowly clerk or downtrodden credit manager, neither of whom is likely, as a mere wage slave, to care two buttons if his boss's firm goes on somebody's blacklist. So put the message on something that more than likely *will* be seen by the big knobs. On the masthead of your printed company stationery. Then the message may strike home.

All important correspondence should go out first-class post. It gets more respect in your postroom and is less likely to get left over to the next day. And remember this: an account £100 overdue for one day may cost you more than the difference in price between a first- and second-class stamp (at 18 per cent per annum), so don't hang on to invoices. Where possible send the invoice with the goods or at least the same day. Most accounting systems are grindingly slow, whether by design or neglect. The more time you give them to digest your bill, the better—for your ulcerated bank manager.

Key correspondence should go by first-class *recorded* delivery. The precaution is not meant to frighten or to be a record in case of emergency—though it is. Formalized, independently documented correspondence has a further salutary effect; your letters are taken more seriously from the outset, your image is subtly enhanced—and so is the likelihood of regular, prompt payment without heartache. The curious thing is that some people who take the precaution of sending mail by recorded delivery fail to mark their letters with this fact. They have not thought through the correspondence process.

The point is that with any sizeable organization, letters come first to a postroom and it is here that recorded and registered post is signed for. The letter then travels through the building to a secretary. She may notice the recorded sticker on the envelope, but she has not actually signed for the letter, so it has no particular impact. When the envelope gets discarded, so does the 'recorded delivery' sticker. The Boss may never be aware that the letter was ever sent by recorded delivery.

For your invoices to do their job properly, they should be vividly marked, hard hitting and unmistakable. Business people handle masses of paper: makes yours stand out.

One of my suppliers, a typist, uses green tinted paper overprinted with the word 'INVOICE' in what looks like purple magic marker. She has a similar letterhead for 'STATEMENT', as a follow-up. But her idea (see Figure 5.5) loses impact. Partly because the word invoice has been printed vertically up the side, involving an acrobatic use of the eyes, and also because 'INVOICE', like the word 'STATEMENT', is too bald.

They are jargon terms, deadened by years of use. What is a statement or an invoice? Ask a business associate. They will invariably use the word 'pay' in their explanation. Of course! That's what it's all about. So get that into your paperwork: 'BILL TO PAY' spells it out. 'BILL STILL TO PAY' is a lot more ominous than the flat statement: 'STATEMENT.'

Queries could be costing your company plenty

As much as a third or even 40 per cent of a company's resources can be tied up in money owing to it. The credit manager who gets results can make a real contribution to profits, easily recouping his salary. What is less well known is that reluctance to pay bills often stems from a query, connected with the invoice, the goods delivered, terms, and so on.

One credit expert is adamant that people overstep their stated terms simply because they don't understand them! You can picture the thought progression:

1. 'What does this mean?'
2. 'If it means. . .I pay early. But if it means. . .I pay late.'
3. 'So I'll pay late and see what happens.'

Why not help remove this potential crick in the system by putting a query phone number and a name to contact on every bill or reminder? Just ask yourself, how many times have you looked at a bill and thought: 'That's not right,' 'Where's the VAT?' or 'What about my last month's credit?'. And so on. And how often have you wanted to phone to clear it up and had to go thumbing through files to find a telephone number that turned out to be the wrong one? It's a frustrating, time-consuming exercise—and time = money.

(In passing, letter carbons can be used as telephone reminders, to help speed up the inevitable call back that follows almost any letter. All you do is type the firm's phone number under their address. When you pull out the carbon of the letter you sent, to refresh your memory, you don't also have to thumb through an address book, or dip into an invoice file.)

Andrew Allies, managing director of Sales Ledger Control Services and a

INVOICE

Maureen Pearson
29 St John's Street
London SE19 3GH

John Lewis
84 Start Hill
London SE9

To typing services for week ending 17.9.78 13 hours @ £1.50	£19.50

Figure 5.5 Invoice

top credit consultant, believes that as much as two-ninths of the cash owing to a firm can be tied up in queries. He lists the essential elements of query control as:

1. The correct recording of a customer query.
2. Swift resolution of the query.
3. Analysis of queries to identify the main cause(s).
4. Investigation of the cause(s) of the query.

Then efforts are made to stop the problem happening again. The customer claim form he recommends has a characteristic design; this details the query. Action needs to be taken fast, and the form must not be mistaken for 'just another office memo'. Other departments provide the collections department with a document flagged with the message 'DO NOT CHASE', indicating that a query investigation is in progress. A customer with what to him is a genuine beef turns into a raging bull when his complaint is ignored.

To speed up the query procedure—and thereby get on with the real game, which is collecting the money—Allies has devised an intriguing little system. It helps give queries an 'artificial priority'. Heads of department are asked to state how long, at most, they will need to resolve particular types of queries. If that time is exceeded, and the query hasn't been cleared up, this is made known *automatically* to someone higher up in the hierarchy. In no time it lands on the desk of the MD. Red faces all round, and everyone starts looking for someone to kick. The result? Queries get swiftly dealt with at the *bottom* of the ladder. Of course allowances are made for especially tricky queries, which may run into extra time.

Spell out how much they owe you

Frequently in dispute is the amount owing. Are your statements doing the best possible job? Do they just show the balance outstanding as a lump sum? Or do they itemize amounts owing and link the sums with the invoice date, reference number, etc. If the customer can pinpoint the 'mistake' fast he'll come back to you fast. But if you send him off to wade through his files to discover how the hell the balance is made up he may put it off for another day or week or month. And meanwhile you wait to be paid. . . and pay to wait.

Adapt your billing system to that of your customer

As I say, it is vital to quote the correct official order number, requisition code, or whatever when invoicing. Some traders have another wrinkle to help slow down the payments they make. The customer needs to apply to the correct office to get paid. One leading British electrical firm operated seven payment offices. If a customer didn't approach the right one, he didn't get paid. Such a scheme can work wonders for cash flow.

Adapt your billing system to that of your customer—that's the key to prompt payment. Find out what triggers payment. Usually it's something simple—ask the customer's bought-ledger department. Some companies need their purchase order number or vendor numbers to process invoices quickly. Find out what is needed—and then make sure that every invoice carries that information.

The error of this omission

Three letters on every bill you send out can cover you against untold pounds' worth of possible mistakes: yours. Do you put 'E & OE' on all your invoices? You should. It stands for 'errors and omissions excepted'. On a £100 bill it means: 'You owe me £100 and I think that's the right figure. But I may have made a mistake and you may really owe me £10000.'

Without E & OE, the customer who pays the £100 for what turns out to be a £10000 item is legally in the clear—and £9900 richer. For an invoice is a legal document; payment is due on invoice and there is technically no need to send out statements, though you may choose to, as summaries or reminders.

Ask—and ye shall receive

Government departments and local councils are notoriously slack payers. The money's there, but they take ages to spew it out. One enterprising builder who knew the problem, and dreaded the effect slow payment would have on his cash flow, asked if there was any special way the council liked to have bills presented. Lo and behold! he was told of a special payments handbook. So while every other supplier on the site bemoaned the inexorable payment delays, *he* rejoiced in regular weekly cash!

Always *ask*. It doesn't take a minute. It could save pounds.

Tips for tradespeople

We British have a horror of asking for money, even when it is rightfully ours. Asking is embarrassing. The Americans are far more brash; but their forthright manner gets results and more money in the bank faster. Andrew Allies explains the psychology thus: 'It's a bit like a salesman not attempting to clinch any sale. A customer who says "no" is a customer lost. But a prospect who hasn't even been asked to buy remains a potential customer.' By not even asking for money the creditor avoids potential problems and the money still feels 'good.'

Allies says that small tradespeople—builders, carpenters, plumbers, electricians—have a bad time of it in the payment stakes. In fact, the better heeled a customer is, the less likely is he to pay the self-employed worker on time. Often a worker will find he's done two or three months' work on one job and then has to wait six months to get paid; three-quarters of a year without remuneration! 'This is primarily the fault of the trader in not agreeing firmly his payment terms,' Allies comments.

Shape up strong from the start: ask to see evidence that the money is there. Take a builder about to accept a commission to erect a home extension. A banker's letter to the customer may detail an overdraft facility; or there may be a second mortgage from a building society and a document to prove it. The customer can still decide to spend the £5000 overdraft on a car for his mistress, but the astute builder's positive attitude may make him think twice.

It is sometimes vital, with protracted work, to agree a payment plan, in advance of starting work, that reduces exposure. For a contractor it might go like this: when all the materials are on site—bricks, window frames, tiles, etc. —20 per cent of the fee is paid; 60 per cent of the money due over the estimated period is forwarded in increments, at agreed points, as progress pay, and the 20 per cent balance paid on completion. This gives the small businessman cash flow and also enables him to cut off if the customer defaults—and not be out of pocket.

If there are alterations to the original specification, these must be agreed in writing, even if it's on the back of a manilla envelope.

How to beat a bankrupt

Credit terms are detailed in Chapter 3. Getting customers to stick to them is more my concern here. Unless trade terms are disputed within a reasonable period it is reckoned that they are acceptable and agreed. But why wait for a further dispute about what constitutes a 'reasonable period'?

J. S. Martin, managing director of Brent (Hailsham) Ltd, sets out his terms of business on a printed sheet 500 words long (see Figure 5.6). He spells it out:

> Where no credit has been opened goods will be despatched C.O.D. or Pro-forma Invoice. Pro-forma invoices are nett.
>
> 4% cash discount 10-days from date of Invoice. Discount taken out of terms will be left as a balance. 2% Credit Surcharge (per month) may be added to overdue accounts after 90 days from date of Invoice. When interest is charged, it will be back-dated and charged from the day the account became overdue.

Manufacturers & Wholesale Distributors of FISHING TACKLE AND ELECTRICAL EQUIPMENT

Brent (Hailsham) Ltd.

Directors J S Martin *(Managing)* J F Martin
Secretary F L Warnes

Registered Office

156, STATION ROAD, HAILSHAM, EAST SUSSEX, BN27 2SA Telephone Hailsham 840094 Telegrams Brent Ltd. Hailsham

Registered in England No. 568303 VAT Registration No. 190 1974 53

TERMS OF BUSINESS

ACCOUNTS: Customers wishing to open an account should give two Trade references and name of Trade Bankers. Where no credit has been opened, goods will be despatched C.O.D. or Pro-forma Invoice. Pro-forma invoices are nett.

CARRIAGE: All orders over £100.00 are sent carriage paid with the exception of goods to the Channel Islands, Ireland and the Isle of Man, where carriage will be paid on all orders over £150.00. Packing materials are included in all carriage charges. LEAD WEIGHTS CARRIAGE EXTRA.

PRICES: All prices are subject to alteration without notice and all orders are accepted at prices ruling on day of despatch.

TERMS OF PAYMENT: 4% cash discount 10-days from date of Invoice. Discount taken out of terms will be left as a balance. 2% Credit Surcharge may be added to overdue accounts after 90 days from date of Invoice. When interest is charged, it will be back dated and charged from the day the account became overdue.

VAN SALES: Our Representative will unfortunately not be able to call on customers who have overdue accounts outstanding.

V.A.T. Must be paid in full as invoiced.

DAMAGE OR LOSS: Please notify the Carriers in writing IMMEDIATELY on arrival, of any loss or damage, and at the same time advise us.

NON-DELIVERY: It is essential that you advise us within 21 days from date of Invoice of non-arrival, to enable us to lodge appropriate claim with the carriers, which, to be valid, must be entered by the senders within 28 days of despatch.

SPECIFICATIONS: Sizes, weights and dimensions quoted are approximate.

SMALL ORDER CHARGE: Orders of £10.00 and under are subject to a minimum carriage and packing charge of £2.00.

OUT OF STOCK ITEMS: Despatched when available unless we are notified in writing to cancel.

COLLECTION OF ORDERS: Customers wishing to collect Orders are requested where possible, to give 48 hours notice of their requirements and thereafter can collect these goods during office hours: Monday to Friday 9.00 a.m. - 12.30 p.m. 1.30 p.m. - 5.00 p.m. A collection discount is allowed where accounts have been settled within our trading terms.

CONDITIONS OF SALE: It is a Condition of Sale of the goods invoiced that they remain the absolute property of BRENT(HAILSHAM)LTD., until the total amount due in respect thereof has been paid.

GOODS RETURNED: Goods returned for Credit are subject to a re-warehousing charge of 15%

Figure 5.6 Terms of business

Could a similar no-nonsense chart tighten up your credit control? Mr Martin also tried getting customers to sign their acceptance of his terms before he would trade with them; this may or may not prove effective in your own line.

Your terms should feature boldly on all quotations, price lists, invoices and statements—then no one can say 'I didn't know.'

Reservation of title: a valuable fail safe

Selling subject to reservation of title sounds complicated. It isn't. And it could save you a packet. By reserving title goods remain your property—even though they have been delivered to the customer—until they have been paid for. The practice was common in Holland and Germany for years. But it was the Romalpa Aluminium Court of Appeal case in 1976 that got UK businessmen thinking about it. A Dutch exporter of aluminium foil had sold to Romalpa Aluminium Ltd under a contract that contained a reservation of title clause. With Romalpa's insolvency, the exporter sued in the English courts for enforcement of this clause against the Receiver. This was the first test for such a clause in England. Its validity was upheld both by the Commercial Court and by the Court of Appeal (*Aluminium Industrie Vaasen BV v. Romalpa Aluminium Ltd.* [1976] 1WLR 676).

Mr Martin tells how one customer was going into liquidation owing him £300. He shot round to the erstwhile customer and discovered that the goods had been placed in the hands of a receiver who was about to auction them. But he managed to identify them, retrieve them and sell what remained for £100, which is better than a third of £nil.

If you want your customers to be bound by a reservation clause you should:

1. Get a good lawyer to draw up a proper reservation of title clause.
2. Get the customer to acknowledge the additional terms.
3. Make sure your goods are clearly marked.

The only fly in this particular balm is that if you do claim reservation of title you can't also claim VAT bad-debt relief (Chapter 10).

How quickly can you clear a cheque?

Cheques are worthy of an entire thesis. Don't take my word for it; read the paperback by Lipman G. Feld, *Bad Checks and Fraudulent Identity: How to Protect Yourself* (National Association of Credit Management, New York, 1978).

There's a lot to be said about cheques. A cheque isn't legal tender; you can refuse to accept it. But a cheque *is* a contract. The cheque writer is saying: 'I have money in the bank to this amount, and just as soon as you can clear this cheque it's yours.' If he hasn't got that money in the bank when you want it that's breach of contract and actionable. And the same applies if he 'stops' the cheque before you reach his bank.

It will pay you, therefore, to clear a cheque as quickly as possible, just in case a cheating client decides to pull out his funds before his cheque can be cleared. If a suspect debtor gives you a cheque ask your bank for special clearance. It costs £1.50 or so, depending on your bank. The bank phones the debtor's branch and confirms that he has the wherewithal to cover the cheque. But the cheque won't be cleared till the morning after—so there's still time for a rogue to stop the cheque or remove his money.

Consider taking an important or worrying cheque right round to the branch on which it is drawn—or get a messenger to do it. You could get the debtor to 'open up' the cheque to 'pay cash.' I got one debtor to write me a little note to go with his cheque, because the more writing the cashier sees in his customer's hand, the less he will worry about possible forgery.

There is another, little known, tactic that will help you clear big cheques fast. Ever heard of Town Clearing? Firms (or private customers) who bank within the City of London will have the letter T in the top right-hand corner of their cheques. It means that, on request, any cheque over £10000 will be taken round on foot (by a bank messenger in a gold-braided uniform) to be cleared on the spot, so saving two days' credit (the usual delay, given the post and clerical time).

However, Town Clearing also works in reverse. And it has been known for big firms purposely not to bank in the City to avoid their own cheques being quickly cleared in this way! With millions of pounds turning over, the saving in a year can amount to a director's salary.

Naturally you will ask to see a cheque guarantee card (guaranteed cheques can't be stopped). You might also look at some other identification that will show a name in full and also an address that you can note. Asking a customer to put his name on a cheque irritates some. But a customer will more readily give his particulars if there is an address section on your receipts. You keep a record on the carbon, of course, but you hand the top copy to the customer. It feels, to him, like he's given away a piece of personal information, but then has got it back again.

At least one major UK retailer gave up asking its staff to rubber stamp the back of the cheque—the stamped grid gives space for name and address, date and so on—because they were too lackadaisical about filling it in properly or even bothering to use the stamp.

What cover does a cheque card really give?

The true value of a cheque guarantee card is known to few. Quite recently I had to pay a removal bill for £138. I offered two cheques for £50 each and one for £38. The removal man was quite satisfied. I don't know why. If those cheques had bounced he would have got paid out by the bank for one only. So he would have got £50? Unlikely. The bank can choose which cheque to honour, and it may choose the £38 one. This is because the guarantee is up to £50 on any *one transaction.*

The conditions on the back of a Lloyds cheque guarantee card state:

> Lloyds Bank Limited guarantees the payment of one cheque only **not exceeding £50** in any single transaction if it:
> (a) is signed in the presence of the payee, the signature corresponding with that on this card;
> (b) is drawn on one of its cheque forms bearing the code number shown on this card and dated before the expiry date of this card.
> (c) has the card number written on the back by the payee.

The banks insist that the card number is written (or mechanically imprinted) on the cheque back by the person accepting the cheque. Because, they reason, at least there is then a fair chance that the shopkeeper or assistant has handled the cheque and, by implication, has also studied and verified the identification details.

The first thing to do with a cheque is check it

Currys, one of the biggest UK electrical retailers, publishes a useful poster for its sales assistants called '4 QUICK CHECKS ON CHEQUES'. These are:

1. Is the date correct?
2. Is the cheque made out to the right party?
3. Do the words and figures agree?
4. Is the cheque signed?

And there are other points to note, such as: never accept a loose cheque (torn from its book) without permission of senior staff; always endorse all receipts in respect of a cheque 'paid by cheque'; make sure the cheque is signed in front of you; that the signature corresponds with that on the bank card; that the bank sorting code (in the centre of the three numbers at the base of the cheque and repeated in the top right hand corner) is the same as the code number on the guarantee card; and that the expiry date hasn't passed.

An unsigned cheque sent through the post is almost always a trick to buy time. It will take perhaps a couple of days for you to send it back, a day in the first-class post getting to the cad, and another week to 10 days before it returns—usually by second-class post.

Cheques on which the date has been wrongly filled in or left off should be dealt with like this. Phone the customer and tell him he's made a mistake. Say you intend to present the cheque and that he should phone his bank branch right away, explaining his error, and asking them to honour the cheque. End-of-year mistakes are common as people invariably put the previous year's date; when a customer gets the year wrong in June, it's the sum, not the sun, that's upsetting him.

Post-dated cheques are a common ruse to get a creditor excited; it makes him feel like he's got a birthday party coming up tomorrow or the week after. But when the cheque bounces and the rigmarole connected with 'kite flying' has been gone through, the client's had another period of free credit.

One fly creditor has no qualms about altering cheques that are wrongly dated. He simply alters them, appends the initials of the payee, and puts it through. It's illegal, but who would pull him up on it? If the debtor tried it could be tantamount to admitting his own attempted fraud.

Never mind whether he's got money in the bank. Does he even own the cheque book?

A cheque is perhaps the shortest form of credit you'll ever agree to. You take it on trust that between accepting it and getting to the bank the debtor stays good for the money. But how do you know he's even good for the cheque book?

In an over-the-counter credit sale, where instant credit is offered, you have to be doubly sure the cheque book isn't stolen. A small cheque-paid deposit could secure a much costlier item. To at least be sure the cheque is right, watch and compare as the customer signs.

Ordinarily a bank clerk is astute enough to see that a cheque is signed in his presence. The presenter then passes across cheque book and guarantee card. You can go one better. Get the guarantee card in your hand first, then let them get on with the signing. If you're worried that the book and card may be stolen and a signature is about to be forged, it surely makes sense not to let the forger have a prompt to hand in the form of the correct signature on the bank guarantee card. When in doubt, get the customer to sign again, on the back of the cheque. Customers don't take offence easily; an honest person respects caution. Only a crook will panic.

Two tricks to watch for

The customer who fakes signing the cheque. He's already forged a passable signature in the quiet of his home, so he shields the cheque with his hand while pretending to write. A cheque card can be 'oversigned'. A heavy pen is used to obliterate the original signature. Because the fake signature is in the crook's own hand he can confidently repeat a signature on the cheque. Always look closely at the signature on the card.

Merely offering something for sale doesn't mean you have to sell it. If you don't like the look of someone's face—or their cheque—you can, as of right, ask them to do the other thing.

Returned cheques

Cheques that come back unpaid from a customer's bank are marked in one of several ways: 'ORDERS NOT TO PAY'; 'WORDS AND FIGURES DIFFER'; **'RD'—refer to drawer; 'RD/PR'—refer to drawer, please re-present**; 'EFFECTS NOT CLEARED.'

You could always remind a customer whose cheques come into the last three categories that he leaves himself open to a criminal charge according to Section 15 of the 1968 Theft Act, the upshot of which is that knowingly issuing a cheque not backed up by funds is fraudulent. The 'knowingly' could be a sticking point in law. But a reminder of the gravity of the failure to clear the cheque is not amiss. Uncleared cheques make damning evidence in court, and this titbit can also be fed to the debtor. In practice, the police usually prosecute if a person has passed three dud cheques. One could be an accident; passing two an error; but three, never!

'Orders not to pay' may indicate that there is an unresolved query on the transaction. But it could be a ploy, a debtor taking an aggressive stance to throw a smokescreen over his real inability to pay. If there is no dispute, then immediate legal action may be the best course, as the company may be on the verge of liquidation.

'Orders not to pay' may mean the Official Receiver is already on the scene. 'Words and figures differ' is a standard delaying tactic, if not an accident (rare). Kill two birds with one stone by phoning the client, telling him he has filled in your cheque incorrectly, that you intend to re-present it and that he should telephone his bank immediately to instruct them to accept the cheque as it is. And add: 'I'll send it through to your bank with a note attached.' If the customer is stalling you'll soon know. Because whereas he might let you put the cheque through and draw a blank again, he is probably not too keen on letting his bank manager know what he is up to and your note would spill the beans.

6. It's happened—they won't pay up: homespun remedies

My own experience with poor payers spans a number of business areas. Apart from journalism and authorship, there's selling pictures, artwork and antiques, publicity work (dealing with designers, photographers, printers), advertising consultancy, and more. The rule of thumb seems to be that the bigger the firm, the slower the payment (hardly surprising when some cheques come through with three signatures on!). According to the Peter Principle (*The Peter Principle*, Bantam, New York, 1970), everyone rises, in business, to their own level of incompetence. Therefore the more 'Indians' there are, the more chiefs there will be—and the more bumbling and cheque writer's cramp you must expect. Another school of thought believes there is a connection between delay in payment and the distance the commissioning principal is from the paying-out unit. Distance, in this case, being numbers of staff, rows of offices, and so on. A corollary runs that the further down the line the cheque issuing and signing function is, the less likely any unpaid and furious individual is to come in and duff up the man who ordered the work. After all, how could non-payment possibly be *his* fault when the cheque-issuing office is three blocks away?

First catch your debtor

It has been wisely said that devious methods of tracing debtors should be reserved for those who have themselves proved to be conspicuously unobtainable. The more dodgy a debtor is, the more justified you can feel about ferreting him out by fair means or foul. But you could certainly start in a relatively benign fashion, as the practitioners of the following methods did. The problem, here, was simply to get the debtor to come to the phone. The more you know about a debtor's private life and amusements, the more effective your 'search and destroy' operations will become. A pools fan will respond like a Porsche 928S Turbo at the start of the standing quarter-mile when the word 'Littlewoods' or 'Vernons' is so much as breathed down the blower, and so many people have Premium Bonds these days that it's a fair bet that if you claim to be phoning from the Premium Bond Headquarters at Lytham St Annes you will similarly have one hotly expectant debtor rushing to the handset.

How much guile—and sheer malice—you put into tracing efforts will, again, depend on how much of a runaround you've suffered at the hands of a debtor. Be assured that the following wrinkles have all had a startling success rate, in spite of the risk of legal action.

You phone up a friend/relative/the office of the debtor and claim that you are from the Clinic for Tropical Diseases and that you are trying to trace Mr Dunabunk to clear him following his recent contact with a person who has subsequently developed typhoid. Another hospital hoax, slightly less devastating: 'I'm phoning from the Almoner's office. We're trying to trace Mr Dunabunk. There's been an accident and we believe he may be able to help. . . .'

The Man from the Ministry (of Funny Stalks, not Walks) has a remarkably successful track record, but you need to know a client's place of work. You phone, ostensibly on a PAYE query, but make sure you talk to a departmental secretary. She has probably been told a dozen times never to divulge a private address to a stranger over the phone, but she cannot resist the authority in your voice, as you say: 'We're trying to check Mr Dunabunk's National Insurance number. It is. . . . Can we verify his address with you?'

Banks are notoriously slack about customer privacy. Not at managerial level, but at the clerical grade, the one you are most likely to reach in a casual phone call to the Current Accounts Department: 'Can you tell me what's been happening to my bank statements. I haven't have one for months. My name's Mr Dunabunk. Where have you been sending them? Are you sure you have the right address? What *do* you have?'

The above is particularly satisfying when I recall that it was a bank manager who told me that he always 'let the punishment fit the crime'. According to the delinquency of a customer he complains to the latter's referees, employer, and finally sends the customer personal scathing letters to his place of work. The letters are marked 'PRIVATE & CONFIDENTIAL', but someone 'forgets' to seal them.

Get his name right before the fight

It is as well to be sure, at the outset, that your work, with its invoice or statement, has in fact arrived. Usually this can be verified at secretary level. If the answer is 'yes', and if the secretary cannot enlighten you about the state of play regarding payment, it is a good idea to discover the name of the chief accounts officer. Names matter.

Have you ever been to a party where the hostess ferries you to the centre of a merry-go-round of grinning strangers, introduces them to you one by one, by names you instantly forget, and then you spend the rest of the evening plucking up the courage to approach one for a chat because you are unable to come up with an opener more scintillating than: 'We were introduced before but I don't remember your name....'?

Names do mean a lot. Ask my assistant. Her name's Gill. But I assumed, for weeks, that her name was 'Jill'. Small matter that I paid my bills promptly. The cheques were made out to 'Jill...'. And that hurt. I hadn't taken the trouble to get it right! She finally put me straight.

So get the name of the person you're talking to on the phone—but not before you've given your own and the name of your company: fair's fair. Get not only the surname but the first name, too. And *write it down*. Don't be fobbed off with initials for the forenames. If the chap is an Algernon or a Caractacus, extract that information. Not only might it help you trace him quickly next time round—Caractacus Smith is easier to locate than one of several Colin Smiths, when you only have a 'C.' to go on—but who knows, one day you may be able to call him 'Crac'. But not before the account hums along....

Having got the chief's name, do not ask to be put through; this merely arouses suspicion in the secretary, which may be communicated to her boss—and invariably, given the poor state of our electro-mechanical hardware, will lead to a disconnected line anyway. No, say a polite thank you, put the phone down, and dial again. With luck, you will discover that your invoice is being processed and there's an end to it. You may still have a month to wait before you can actually finger the cheque, but you are in the final furlong.

'He's in a meeting'

Danger signs are when you know that the boss's secretary recognizes your voice and knows why you are phoning up as you give your name, but even before you state your business. You can sense the handset twisting in her sweaty palm. Bosses who are always in conference ('in a meeting' is the standard expression), out of the room, interviewing, gone to lunch, working from home, or in another part of the building are likely trouble-makers.

The most effective ploy here is to pretend to be somebody else. To avert suspicion, co-opt your secretary or get a woman friend to pretend to be your secretary. 'Hello, is that Mr Smith's office...I have Mr...for you'. Secretaries like talking to secretaries; it somehow confirms the justness of the system and their own importance within the hierarchy. But who should you decide to be? Ideally, someone you know Mr Smith will want to talk to; perhaps one of his major customers or his advertising agent. Often as not, Mr Smith, who three minutes before was 'out of the office' or 'in a meeting', miraculously reappears. You then say who you really are and state your business. As he blusters, blame his secretary for any misunderstanding; blame her apparent deafness, if you want. You may even hear the poor chap rattling his bottle of blood pressure pills!

If this fails, because your fraud is discovered, or because the debtor is genuinely absent, then leave clear instructions for him to phone you back. When next you phone, if you have not yet been contacted, the secretary—who certainly knows that her boss did not return your call (and probably knows why as well)—will begin to feel like an unwilling accomplice, and this can be detected in her tone. What you are trying to discover is how far things have gone or are likely to go. Is it to be an easy matter, securing your rightful payment? Or is a major siege operation called for?

It's never too soon to phone

Even if you're a rotten conversationalist, a timorous payment chaser, you can become a first-rate listener: silence at this stage is golden. Note the details of any query; promise it will be dealt with swiftly, do it, and then get smartly back to the customer.

When should you start phoning a client? A week or 10 days after he lets you down for payment? Not necessarily. In the most forward-looking accounts departments, phone calls begin *even before the account is due.* An experienced telephone talker can find out, in the course of an apparently spontaneous chat, whether the goods arrived on time, without damage, whether they were satisfactory (it may even be possible to win a reorder there and then from a satisfied customer), and close with: 'So we can expect to get your cheque on... (the due date).'

Once the due date has passed, any time is a good time to phone—the sooner, the better. You want to know quickly what the problem is; only then can you begin your rearguard action for speedy collection.

Although phone calls can be 'fielded away' by a clever talker, at least you are aware that it's being done at that very instant. Letters—even welcome ones—often languish unread and even unopened in 'IN' trays for weeks. But if your telephone call does make contact with the right person it is a relatively easy matter to pin someone down to a clear statement of intent.

The most effective way to handle a 'pay up' conversation is not to work your way up to the real reason for the call, beginning with trivia or subsidiary business. First, make sure you have the right person on the line; say who you are; then, in short sentences, say why you are phoning. A typical script might read: 'Mr Symonds? Johann Sebastian Bach here. I'm the guy who composes your weekly cantata. I'm still waiting for payment of my March account. You had the bill four months ago. Would you mind telling me when I can expect to be paid?' Try to avoid any kind of discussion. You don't want to know *why* payment is late; that's a standard stalling tactic. All you need to know is *when you are going to get the cheque.*

Vagueness is a foretaste of trouble. The fog usually descends when talk turns to sending the cheque. Typical woolly responses are: 'I'll look into it'; 'We'll get round to it'; 'I'll do it sometime this week/by the end of the week.' Counter this with 'Mr...I made a special effort to talk to you personally so we could work together to avoid any further delay with payment of my account. As you can see, you're already over our agreed terms. I have to be sure when I can expect to receive your cheque....'

When closing a dunning conversation, it's as well to keep coming on strong, right through the last furlong. You not only get the customer to agree that he will send a cheque right away, but also add that you will phone to confirm that it has arrived. He can hardly say: 'Don't bother, I didn't mean what I said about sending the cheque.' He'll have to agree to expect your call. What you are really saying, of course, is: 'If you don't send the cheque as and when you say, I'm going to stay on your back.'

Then, and only then, should you launch into any other business. Often a few words about another project settles the tangy aftertaste of your previous request. But don't fade out into niceties at the end of the call. In a sales letter, the PS, the last minute reminder, carries an enormous clout. You can get a similar effect over the phone. Remind the person you are talking to why you phoned: 'So you will get that cheque to me by...?'

Standard telephone stalling tactics—and how to tackle them

A first-contact call when an account has passed its due date may draw the response: 'I'll look into it.' Why not shove the onus back on the debtor by saying: 'Fine, I'll hold on'?

'I've just made out a cheque'; 'Your cheque's in the post'; and 'Your cheque will be made out today', are designed to be like Muzak to your ear; the debtor hopes the soothing effect of money words will send you into a trancelike state of optimistic anticipation. Don't let it happen. Your response should be: 'Oh good, how much for?' It can be a part of some professional procrastinator's art to pay a portion of a bill and wait for the customer to complain. (And someone who has just signed, or is about to sign, a cheque should have no excuse for not knowing the true amount. Ask for the cheque number, too.)

The question 'how much for' will also sort out a fairly recent cost-cutting exercise certain businessmen are practising. They leave off the VAT, even though a VAT registration number is clearly marked on correspondence. Remind anyone who does that to you that as much as you are obliged by law to charge VAT so is he obliged to pay it.

Proof of delivery requests—'Are you sure the goods were sent?'—and requests for copy invoices must, for a while at least, be taken at face value. Send what is asked for, at once. And make a special effort to discover what went wrong. It could be you are not putting on your invoices a requisition number or some other identifying mark that the customer's accounts system requires. Give clients no excuse for non-payment—then, if they do develop palsy of the purse-strings, you can hit them with everything you've got, with no niggling doubts.

Now you can see the usefulness of jotting down, in shorthand, the excuse given for non-payment. You can quickly 'blow the cover' of a customer who favours the same excuse every month. A bit of sarcasm is not out of place: 'Which copy invoices would you like this month?' should have a suitably aperient effect...

Taped evidence—damning indeed

It may be a good idea to tape the phone call. Taped evidence is just beginning to be admitted in British courts, so that if you ever approach that dreaded endgame, a mention that you have a tape-recorded version of key statements—absolute corroboration of the damning evidence—you may well be rewarded with a swift about-turn and a cheque in the post.

Many people live in a kind of unspoken, even unthought-about fear that they are being bugged. If you don't believe it, mention to a good friend that you taped a recent phone call with them. Then try to reassure them that you didn't really. (On second thoughts, maybe you should try it with a casual, expendable acquaintance....) For the truth is that most people gab without thinking—which is why, when a taped interview is typed up and read back to an interviewee, he will so often deny or contradict something that he has verifiably just said.

The best time of day to telephone

A regular phone call can have the same kind of abrasive effect as a certain kind of roughage-rich breakfast cereal taken in daily doses. A constipated accounts department may be similarly moved to produce the cash, after the requisite number of doses. But when is the best time to phone? Most office staff, including executives, are at their desks by a particular time every morning; it may be pride in work, an obsessional streak, a symbolic doffing of the cap to vigilant authority, or sheer necessity to a card-punching time-server. Nevertheless, most people have a settling-in period, during which they empty their briefcases, fiddle with paperwork, refold the newspaper or drink the first cup of tea of the work day. That is the best time to catch them. Before duty calls, before the secretary wafts in with her letter pile, before the Big Boss makes his presence felt. Find out what that time is and use it to your own advantage.

Which day should you choose? Monday may well be the best day of the week to catch sluggardly payers off guard. People relax after the weekend; they forget the trauma of the week gone by and one to come. And, most people start a task—in this case the working week—on the right foot. I would hazard a guess that more people are at their desks, on time, on a Monday, than on any other day of the week.

Telephone techniques

The Monday morning approach is fine for the first-time contact with a slow payer. But the confirmed slow payer needs a more random approach to time—any time of the day or week, without warning—or else he will come to expect your regular call and work out a means of fielding it away.

Call preparation is a must. The customer history card (Figure 6.1) shows how a professional organization like Sales Ledger Control Services approaches the task. The facts must be at your fingertips. Your firm's business is your priority. But the person on the other end of the line has a different priority: his business. Have ready the account/reference number *he* knows you by. Make his life easy and maybe he'll return the favour. Besides, an interrupted conversational flow, while you trace unclear details of the account, will seriously dent your image. Not only will you have trouble picking up the threads, the interval having killed your patter, but you'll also have a devil of a job getting the person back to the line once he knows what's coming.

As with almost every sort of 'freelance' activity (defined as an activity in which the financial outcome is unsure, only time and effort expended being guaranteed) it pays to move quickly. The chances of getting to grips with more than a couple out of, say, 10 debtors, over the phone, in any one session is remote. But until you get started you won't know which ones are available. A personal shorthand system for keeping track of the results helps. A fairly orthodox code might look like this:

AD – Account disputed
NL – Phone number not listed

CUSTOMER'S NAME .... ACCOUNT No. .... TELEPHONE No. ....

ADDRESS ....

INVOICES TO .... QUERIES TO ....

CONTACT NAME .... POSITION .... TYPE ....

M.A. NAME .... TITLE .... TYPE ....

BUYER .... TEL. No. .... TERMS: STANDARD/OTHER ....

DATE OF CALL	BALANCE CHASED	RESULT						OTHER COMMENTS
		CL.PD.	C.I.P.	DATE	QUERY	REF.	FOLLOW-UP	

Figure 6.1 Customer History Card. (This card is designed by, and is copyright of, Sales Ledger Control Services)

RC – Recall
LM – Left message
TCMB – To call me back (+when)
CIP – Cheque in post
PIF – Paid in full
PP – Part payment
CIR – Copy invoice requested
CIS – Copy invoice sent
PODR – Proof of delivery requested
PODS – Proof of delivery sent
PC – Payment claimed
CW – Company going to the wall
RIP – Receiver invited to participate
GT – Gone trace, gone away
LA – Legal action indicated
SL – Solicitor's letter sent (+when)
SS – Stop supplies
WO – Written off
LR – Letters returned
CSA – Cheque signatory absent
PP – Payment promised
Q – Query
OS – Order stopped pending payment
NR – No reply
TUC – Telephone up creek

You might like to add a few of your own, such as BF and SC.

Telephone handling of broken promises

What if a promised cheque does not materialize? Begin your follow-up phone conversation like this: 'Did you make out that cheque we spoke about last week? I didn't get it.' He is an innocent party, you imply; obviously the cheque has got snarled up in the office system, but it is up to him, to 'close the matter'. Use clichés: it has a reassuring, deadening effect, like the peaceful drone of a crocodile of monks disappearing down the corridor of a monastery. It is also in marked contrast to what you say next, so there is shock value as well. 'So there shouldn't be any problem now. . . .' He makes the right sort of verbal nodding noises. 'And you won't mind if I save your company considerable time and trouble and come in and pick up a cheque in person?' For some reason this appears to have the same effect as tipping a bottle of Snowpake down a navy blue pinstripe suit. It concentrates attention wonderfully. For as long as a troublesome creditor can be batted away over the phone, fobbed off with anodyne letters, or (more likely, given the cost of the post and office time) silence, he does not really exist. Business people are happy to stitch up suppliers, to keep them waiting for payment, in absentia, as it were. But talk about coming in and you, the creditor, become, not a disembodied voice, not an integer, but a *person*. And never mind whether you are built like a rhino or a reed, the awesome image is not a fisticuffs threat but an emotional threat; the trauma of a confrontation which might result in a *scene*. And this, if it involved other staff members, could entail *loss of face*. So the good chance is that you will be swiftly paid.

Can a woman work wonders?

Depending on your own sensitivity for your particular occupation, the disposition of the people you are dealing with, the size of their organization, and so on, you will be able to judge whether the sequence of phone calls should be an extended one, or telescoped with your threat of a personal visit being made after only a couple of calls. You may find it effective to have someone else phoning up on your behalf. Curiously, a woman is less likely than a man to offend a man, possibly because she does not pose the man-to-man physical threat. The reverse might also be true, for reasons of sex; a mellifluous male is able to charm a swift response from a slow female cheque-signer.

A credit consultant friend, and telephone-collection expert, opts for a different explanation for the female's telephonic effectiveness. He agrees, she *can* be more conciliatory, but offers pragmatic reasons, not fancy Freudian ones. He says that although telephone collection is interesting—and certainly challenging—work, it does not have a career structure to appeal to an ambitious man. Consequently, at a given salary, at a given clerical level, the chances are that a female telephone collector is of a higher calibre than a male. The consultant's prime telephone operatives are married women with children; mature, settled people who are not looking for promotion. In contrast, women believe any sort of debt collecting—even on the phone—is easier done by men. Women often assume, presumably because of a non-feminist upbringing, that a man carries more authority as of right.

Keep mum about dad's debts

Telephonic dunning has one serious drawback: that of bringing into the picture someone who has no right to know about the overdue account. Nobody but the clerk in an accounts department, who has the file under his nose, the principal partner, his accounts controller, or a company director should be party to the details of an overdue account. The fear is of involving an outsider, like the debtor's wife or mistress. Making known the details of a debt could lead to action under the Administration of Justice Act, Section 40 (see page 4), if it could be construed that communicating the information to a third party was designed to put pressure on the debtor. 'Unlawful harassment' could be the courtroom interpretation.

A salesman who walked into a debtor's office and proceeded to shoot off his mouth to the receptionist about how much money her boss owed his boss soon found himself in big trouble. A debtor director overheard the conversation, phoned the salesman's managing director and insisted he come over at once and sort out his loud-mouthed salesman. The salesman was duly carpeted and the managing director threatened with legal action. Was the bill not truly seriously overdue? Oh, yes. But that is immaterial in law. The debtor company had gained some unwarranted ammunition, and boy, did they use it—to gain more time and steal some more credit!

Payment chasing through the post

A phone call that leads to payment is sweet; telephone calls get lost in the ether. That's why you may prefer to get satisfaction over the phone. There's more chance of keeping your client amenable to future business, should you wish it. Letters are a concrete record of your trouble-making nature—and a permanent burr in the saddle of the debtor's conscience. But a dunning letter may become a necessity.

The do-it-yourself dunning letter

If ever you needed professional-looking headed stationery, it is now. Keep your missive short—remember, this is bad news. The inclination will be to file it—possibly in the wastebin. Another tip: give it a title. '500 WIDGETS SUPPLIED BY H. ARDUP & COMPANY TO S. LOWPAYERS LTD. PAYMENT QUERY.'

Your headline can gain in truculence as the days draw in and your temper wears thin: 'BILL TO PAY,' 'BILL STILL UNPAID' can follow your standard title. Most people are terribly inattentive readers and quickly bored. Get to the point with short sentences. A paragraph need be no more than a single sentence. The point of a title is that it will always get read. Not many people read all of the items in a newspaper or every advertisement in a publication, but they do take in the titles. Indeed, it is on the strength of the title that they decide whether or not to delve further. The same applies to letters.

Humour, in the text, can also be a good idea—as long as the wit is barbed. When a big-name advertising agency commissioned me to write a mail-order advertisement, and then didn't pay me for three months, I wrote:

> Dear Mr Blank
>
> Do you know the 'laws' of mail order?
>
> One of them states that once the customer has paid up, you get the goods to him right away.
>
> Over the weekend of March 23 I was asked to write an ad for your company—and get it to your office by Monday morning. I met that deadline.
>
> That was three months ago. I have yet to be paid!

Their cheque arrived two days later. I had touched a nerve, wounded professional pride, perhaps.

It often helps to spell things out in a letter. Tell your debtor what you said; remind him of his reply. Tell him the date of correspondence. Remember, anything that involves a bit of research on his part, a hunt through his files, slows up the payment process. Worst of all, it gives your quarry an excuse to put off looking. And he may well pass the task over to a minion whose own priorities and prejudices swing into action and will also help to gum things up. Try, in your copy, to elicit sympathy: You may have a VAT problem. Say that legally, VAT becomes payable from the date an invoice is despatched. If a payment cheque is not received promptly, VAT will need to be paid in advance of settlement. In other words, you are subsidizing the government, thanks to him. If this is merely a slow payer, not a determined non-payer, plucking at his heart strings may do the trick.

There are a number of ways of boosting the explosive power of your prose. I recently sent the following letter:

> Dear Miss B...
> RECORDED DELIVERY
>
> PROFESSIONAL SERVICES: £133 OUTSTANDING
>
> I spoke to you on March 8, 1980, when you agreed to send me a cheque for £133 (including VAT) without further delay. Since then I have heard nothing. You said you would send the money right away.
>
> If the cheque is not received within 48 hours I shall have no alternative but to place the matter in the hands of the County Court WITHOUT FURTHER NOTICE TO YOU.
>
> A summons will then be issued against you and you could well be ordered to pay me the money, together with my costs.
>
> It is therefore in your own interest to settle this business without further delay.

I prefer to threaten with immediate court action, but you can send a solicitor's letter first. However, I feel that this is a kind of halfway house to the doom-laden corridors of the courts. A solicitor is himself a trades person, albeit a respected, well-paid one. Nevertheless he can also be side-stepped—witness the numbers of solicitors who are themselves frequently 'knocked' by their clients. A committed, wealthy non-payer may be delighted to invoke his own legal eagle, to take the burden of responsibility off his own shoulders. Once solicitors start talking to solicitors, you are usually a million more miles from payment of the bill in dispute—but close to receiving a fresh bill: the one your solicitor sends you.

If poor payers are a regular and unavoidable part of your business (happy is the man or woman who can afford to deal only with people who pay up on the button), you could consider having printed some special dunning stationery. As a debt-collecting agency chief said, the dunning letter is the prime tool of his trade. Usually it is a combination of feints and ambiguous threats that often amount to nothing. It is also important to make the letter look 'cyclostyled'. The less personal it is, the more chilling the effect. Thus, boldly printed in red comes the strapline

FINAL NOTICE

(In ordinary black type, there follows:)

Dear Sir/Madam

(The trick is not to bother deleting whichever applies, as a kind of signal that the niceties no longer need to be observed. The letter continues, in black type:)

RE: AMOUNT OUTSTANDING OF £... PAYABLE TO...

(Not many people know what 'RE' means. But they know it's formal and frosty. To further distance the reader, continue in the following vein:)

We wish to give you formal notice that *unless this amount is received at these offices within 72 hours of receipt of this letter, legal proceedings will be instituted to recover the full amount due, together with any legal costs which you may be required to bear.*

Payment should be returned with this letter in the enclosed envelope, made payable to our client. First-class postage is advised.

Yours faithfully

...

CREDIT INSPECTOR

(No one knows what a 'Credit Inspector' is, but it sounds nasty, and the signature above it is suitably illegible. But be sure your switchboard knows whom to pass the call to when the 'Credit Inspector' is wanted!)

Because the Office of Fair Trading now licenses debt-collection and credit-reference agencies, the wording of the letter needs to be such that it does not misrepresent or appear to come from a company or organization that does not exist or is not registered. But obviously, if you can use a different address from your own, this is a definite plus.

Of course, if you need to have special letters printed to dun poor payers, you may start wondering whether you are in the wrong business. If your problem is occasionally to trace a hard-to-pin-down person who owes you money, the odd telegram may be all that is needed. The trick is to profit—literally—from the curiosity of the human animal. Who, for example, could ignore the following note from the Express Parcel Services' delayed-delivery department?

Dear Sir/Madam

Would you please be good enough to telephone the above number in respect of an undelivered insured parcel?

Please quote the docket number given above and your name and address when telephoning. Please telephone from Monday to Friday. You may reverse the charges only between the hours of 1 pm and 5.30 pm. Please do not telephone on Saturday and Sunday or on Bank Holidays as this office is closed.

Another, often effective, written reminder can be used. This carries a threat, not of legal action, but an appeal to a higher authority. First find out to whom your cheque signer is responsible, by name. And preferably go a step further, too: find out the name of the latter's master—even if you are now talking about the chief executive or chairman of the board. A polite letter is then called for stating that you expect immediate satisfaction but that if that is not forthcoming, it may be necessary to contact so-and-so direct. Most bosses will stand firm with their subordinates; after all, they are usually in general agreement about trading policies and your unpaid bill is unlikely to be unique. Nevertheless, mere hirelings do not like to have to explain themselves to the big boys. Nor, after the event, do they care to be beholden to their lords and masters for having been extricated from a tight spot. So you may be in with a winning ploy here.

The fake bill that gets 'em running

The reminders sent out in a collection cycle are so often dull, routine documents, so obviously 'form' or stereotype letters that they may even be numbered, so the debtor knows how far advanced he is in the series! Is it any wonder they're quickly filed, and often in the wastepaper bin? One enterprising collector mulled over this problem by asking himself the question: 'What makes me pay up?' The answer came back: 'Not a lot!' But he did remember what had made him leap to the phone at least to contact the creditor, usually the gas, phone or electricity people. It was when they sent him someone else's huge bill in error. He tried it on a few slow payers, sending them fictitious reminders with some extra noughts thrown in. Instead of his having to chase them for payment, they were jamming up his switchboard soon after the post had arrived, desperate to sort things out!

A fairly recent non-paying manoeuvre involves VAT. The net bill is paid, but the VAT element is omitted. A phone call to the accounts office stating your VAT registration number, the amount outstanding, and a reminder of the nature of the bill and the relevant dates may be sufficient. The next step is to remind the culprit that VAT is payable by law. If this fails to work, the debt can be tackled in any of the above ways. In my line of work, it is often possible to tack the missing amount on to the next bill, together with a further amount to take into account VAT for the latest bill. It's naughty, but it's nice. And everyone gets what they deserve, don't they?

Most debts do not remain unpaid because of lack of money; the most common reason for non-payment is sloth—allied to cussedness. But occasionally there can be genuine cash-flow problems, especially where the person who owes the money is a private individual or in business in a small way. Here it can be effective to offer to reduce the debt by, say, 20 per cent. After all, better 80 per cent of something than 100 per cent of nothing.

Adjust the amount you are prepared to forfeit in inverse proportion to the likelihood of your receiving anything.

A debtor's instalment plan

What if the customer offers to pay off the account? It may happen and be the best offer you'll get. So be prepared; work out, in advance, what you want to or can afford to accept. But before breathing a word of your own considered instalment plan ask: 'What do you have in mind?' The suggestion may be more favourable to you than your own estimated pay plan. The deal can be further loaded in your favour by asking for a little time to think it over. If you talk in the morning, call back in the afternoon with your answer; if you phone in the afternoon, get back to the customer first thing next morning. And if you talk on a Friday, get the client's home number and phone him on Saturday morning. There's nothing like showing that special favours demand special concessions all round. A little inconvenience will demonstrate to the client that he has broken a rule of business (never mind that it's being broken all the time), and must expect to have his own smooth routine jangled a little.

You then reject whatever has been suggested. Not out of hand, but with sufficient disdain to enable you to tighten the screw a bit. So if the offer on a debt of £300 was for £50-a-month repayments over six months, suggest £150 cash up front and three post-dated cheques of £50, one for each of three months. Weighing up all the factors you may conclude that you deserve (and can get) some interest, too. Try it and see. When you get agreement stay on the offensive; ask the client to put your 'understanding' in writing and to send the cheques with his letter. If the letter doesn't arrive in a short while, send him a letter confirming your arrangement. Send this (and every other scrap connected with a tardy payer) by first-class recorded delivery stating on the letter that it is 'RECORDED DELIVERY'. Phone to confirm your letter has arrived. Press for the cheques and a note confirming acceptance of the terms contained in your letter. *Push, push, push; and they may pay up.*

If any of these cheques bounce it is time to get heavy. Remind the client that he is risking prosecution under the provisions of Section 15 of the 1968 Theft Act concerning criminal fraud. Payment at this stage must mean nothing less than crinkly cash, a telegraphed money order, or a telephoned bank transfer—and *tout de suite*. Cheques that are wrongly completed should not be sent back for alteration; that'll mean another two weeks' free loan of your money. Just phone the signatory and say: 'You've obviously made a mistake. Please write to your bank and tell them to expect this cheque and to clear it.' The duff cheque writer can hardly say it was *supposed* to be a cock-up. He'll march to orders—you hope.

Calling a debtor's bluff

Occasionally you meet the 'honest' debtor who says, straight out: 'Sorry, we've got a cash-flow problem. We just can't pay you this month. But if you can hold on till....'' First remind yourself that it's precisely to avoid snaring *yourself* in the cash-flow cesspit that you're chasing him. Then say, as poker-voiced as possible: 'That's tough. You have my sympathy. More than that, though, I'd like to help. When would be a good time for me to come in and go through the books with you? I don't see why we can't help you out, once the position is clear....' If you want to be really nasty, suggest having your accountant or company secretary in tow.

Stopping supplies can have a salutary effect on a slothful payer. It depends on how strong your position is in the market; he may be able to buy similar goods or services elsewhere. And there is always the risk of hastening the demise of a company by curtailing their ability to keep on trading and hopefully pull themselves, eventually, out of the mire.

An alternative last-resort manoeuvre is to get the proprietor or a director of a struggling concern to give a personal guarantee. Your argument goes like this: any bank would want to take a charge on some asset to back a loan or substantial overdraft; effectively you are acting as a bank in granting extended credit, therefore you, too, are justified in taking a charge (only unencumbered private assets need be considered: there's a limit to how many ways you can cut a cake). A willingness to pledge possessions is always a good sign. The debtor offers to underwrite his own confidence in the future—and you can't ask for, or expect, better than that.

Payment in kind

In that rare circumstance in which your bill remains unsettled because of genuine lack of cash, you may yet profit from your loss: suggest payment, not in cash, but in kind. Supposing a television retailer owes you £100, you could suggest that he gives you a TV set of equivalent value. His profit margin might be anything up to 30 per cent, so he might consider he has done well out of the deal. You could let him off with more of a bump by pitching your bid a little higher, say a set worth £120, and the retailer is still quids in on his original debt. Spell out the advantages. He increases his turnover, still makes a small profit, and his cash-flow situation is unimpaired. A further plus, far from having wrung a cheque out of him, you have put business his way, show a willingness to continue your trading association, and you are more likely to be offered work in the future. Having got his agreement verbally, get him to put it in writing. If the letter doesn't arrive quickly, *you* confirm the 'understanding,' by recorded delivery.

Telegrams are sometimes effective where letters have failed to find their target, or have not produced a response. Telegrams do not get opened, normally, by anyone other than the person to whom they are addressed. A telegram is regarded with a mixture of terror and respect, so you can assume that it will be correctly ferried to your quarry. You also know that there is a record of your message, should it be needed in court. Allied to a telegram, is the rather more dramatic remedy adopted by a Frenchman nursing an unpaid bill. The man, who had influential friends, sent the cheque-signer a wreath of flowers with the message attached: 'Please pay me the money you owe me, or RIP your reputation.'

Getting paid through a 'punch-up posture'

It is against the law to frighten physically those who are remiss in paying their bills, so weight-lifting friends or Great Dane owners cannot be co-opted. But that does not mean you cannot hit people in their conscience. A friend of mine was having severe trouble with a cheque-signer with writer's cramp. Being unmarried, he got an actress acquaintance with a small baby to pose as his distressed wife. The girl, hamming it up all the way, arrived at the director's office, bawling babe in arms. The gist of her plea was that she would have to drown the baby if the bill was not paid, because they were stony broke, the landlord was trying to evict them, and the baby, which she at that point thrust forward, was ill with mumps. It was a fair bet that the man was aware of the possible side effects of mumps, but had forgotten, if he ever knew, that only pre-teen males are seriously at risk of sterility. As a result, not only was he made to feel guilty about the outstanding debt, but he also wanted to get rid of the screaming threat to his manhood as fast as possible!

Not every ploy will work, not even if you run through the whole gamut. But all your efforts should be concentrated on winning 'in the jungle'—without recourse to law. Once you need to use a solicitor or the small-claims court, or a higher court, rather than merely *threaten* litigation, you are into a grey area with different ground rules. No longer are you master of your own fate. Solicitors' fees are formidably high, and even if you win with costs, no account is made of your own time, and energy, which is always better employed in a forward march, furthering your own business interests, rather than fighting a wearying rearguard action.

One small word of warning: be sure of your facts along the way. On one occasion, after months of trying to extract a cheque from a company, after a stream of letters, from the polite to the openly hostile, had failed to work, and when all of my key targets were conspicuously absent whenever I phoned, I decided to pay the cheque-signer a visit.

I dressed in 'bundle' gear, the sort of clothes in which one would not think twice about rolling on the ground and fighting in, if it came to it. Not that I had any intention of fighting, but the visual message would be transmitted and could well enhance my aggressive posture.

Fortunately the office was a big open plan one, by far the best arrangement for embarrassing the person I had come to see. I was asked to wait in an anteroom. So I waited. And waited. And waited some more. Then I pinpointed my prospect, and noticed that the door to the inner sanctum, in which he sat surrounded by staff, had an automatic catch on it. Anyone who had not been buzzed through would be automatically locked out. (Needless to say, I surmised from this little gadget that they were used to uninvited guests and had taken precautions.) However, I also spotted that the door-closing mechanism had a slight delayed action; if I dashed in behind a visitor who had been allowed through, I would just manage to nip in before the door closed.

This I did. I strode up to the nasty man who had been screwing me up for months and buttonholed him, in a loud voice: you can make an awful lot of fuss, I discovered, about throwing off the hand of a chap who tries to elbow you out of an embarrassing situation—embarrassing for him, that is.

Eventually, I agreed to go and wait—for 10 minutes—while he organized the cheque. I made it clear that I would be back in again if it wasn't ready on time. It was, and, a little shaken, I was out into the fresh air, cash in hand—or so I thought. In fact I had made two mistakes,

My first mistake was not having asked to have the cheque 'opened up' and made out to 'pay cash,' because a cheque is as easily stopped as it is made out. This I remedied by going straight to the firm's own bank branch, which was conveniently near, and getting the company to verify, over the phone, that cash could be paid.

The second mistake was really luck, or rather unluck, of the draw. About a week later, a cheque came through the post, for the amount I had winkled out of the company. It had been correctly made out to me, for the right amount, and my name and address had been accurately filled in on the pay slip. However, someone had typed the wrong address on the envelope, and it had been several weeks in limbo finding my own letter-box. I had dunned an innocent man. Or had I?

7. The professional collectors

Do you need a collection agency? How do they work? What do they charge? Which one should you choose? These are questions that the credit manager or proprietor must answer. You may need at least to try the effect of an agency on sticky debtors if your own efforts take too long to work. Collection takes up valuable company time, or even executive time, which is far better spent creating wealth rather than pulling in what is rightfully yours.

But before you even consider an agency, try this little test suggested by a top credit consultant. 'If you've been sending out a series of letters and the customer only pays up when you write threatening legal action with letter six, then send the bugger the sixth one first!'

The most appealing agencies to use are those that don't charge for failures: 'No collection—no fee' is the usual slogan. It's worth bearing in mind, in this context, that in-house collection exercises, successful or otherwise, are financed out of company profits and there is unlikely to be the same degree of do or die incentive in a credit clerk who will get paid whether he wins or not.

Some say a debt should be passed to an agency a week or two weeks after it is past due, though an agency may prefer you to wait until your gamut of company letters has gone out, dunning phone calls made, and so on, before wading in. But it's true that the longer a debt remains outstanding, the harder it is to collect. And never mind the so-called psychological reasons for this—the debtor gets hardened in his resolve, bolder in his intransigence with every inch given. Just look to the facts, readily available from the lips of many a businessman: an old debt is a deathbed debt. While waiting to be paid, don't hold your breath.

The voucher system of credit help: You pay first, dun later

As well as the no collection–no fee agencies, there is the fairly recent American favourite, the voucher system. A company buys a book of collection vouchers and sends one back with completed details of the debtor. The entitlement is usually to a series of letters, each getting stiffer, that continues for several weeks.

If that doesn't work, telephone collection or personal visits may be offered, for a further fee or percentage of cash collected. The end-of-the-road legal action is also often handled by the big agencies' solicitors. The success rate of agency legal eagles astonishes some, but is explained by two things: first, the fact that such retained lawyers (they may even be based in the same building as the agency) spend so much time dealing with debts that they know all the tricks; and second, the agency has by this time established the validity of the debt and has the full documentation presented in a way the courts prefer.

Your best advice on which agency to choose often comes from a trusted friend, preferably in a similar line of business. Some agencies not only pull in the money, but the cash also passes through their hands before being transferred to the creditor, minus charges. You want to be sure you are not going to be chasing a dodgy credit-collection agency as well as a debtor! But how? Audited accounts must be seen; evidence of employee bonding is also reassuring; and because you probably want to continue trading with your debtor, you'll need to see the ammunition the agency intends to use—its letters, an outline of its telephone approach, the tone adopted, etc.

Keep a record of the efficiency of the agency you choose, how long they take to get back your money and pass it on (some agencies do not handle a client's recovered funds; they get the debtor to send it direct to you), and how much they charge all told—including your own and your staff's time spent in communication. Remember: bringing in a third party is either a cost-effective exercise or why bother?

All the evidence suggests that the 'ingredient X' that makes the professional collection agencies triumph where others teeter is almost incidental to any expertise they may or may not have in debt collecting. They are a third party, outsiders to the curious, sometimes almost intimate, relationship that develops between creditor and debtor. Even at street level the phenomenon exists. A veteran foot-in-the-door debt collector told me the trick was to 'smash 'em and schmooze 'em'—Yiddish for suck up to somebody. 'If people owed you money you were bound to end up friends with them,' he insists.

The explanation is simple. Most often the debtor is quite aware that a due date has passed. He knows he's keeping back the money. And the creditor certainly knows he hasn't got *his* money. Yet he also knows that he will get it eventually; only a relatively small number of debts—even those left to moulder—will actually go bad, i.e., become uncollectable. What ploy the creditor can use to get his cash a bit quicker becomes a challenge. And so a kind of game develops, a game of catch the rat. Bringing in an outsider, the agency, is like hiring a terrier. Then the message to the debtor is clear: the game has escalated.

Credit agencies

The following series of credit agency profiles is not exhaustive. It may not even be representative. What is significant, however, is that the companies mentioned advertise extensively and produce a wealth of helpful, often free, literature. Modern civilization has yet to diminish the apparently irresistible human urge, when someone sticks his neck out, to knock his block off. High profile companies carry their reputation as a pennant, and in this consumer-coddling society there may be some valid reason for equating the brave with the good.

The Credit Protection Association Limited

David Lee Barber, national sales manager of the Credit Protection Association, introduced himself and his company with the following scene-stealing opening shot: 'Whilst we are probably the oldest established debt collecting agency in this country [65 years], this is 1981 and for the last four years we have changed our image. No longer do we consider ourselves debt collectors but rather we provide a service to deal with overdue accounts. In business, delaying payment for as long as you can is everyone's favourite game; but we can think of no reason whatever why a person supplying goods should not be able to rely on being paid in accordance with his credit terms. The message is a simple one—*the name of the game is cash flow.*'

An important aspect of their new method of operations is that although the psychological advantages of a 'third-party approach' are enjoyed, the debtors' goodwill is still retained. And the reason is that the debtors are asked to pay directly to the client and not to CPA. That way debtors are allowed to feel that they have paid of their own free will and this is conducive to a normal amicable relationship being maintained. Of course it also means that CPA's clients get their money quicker than if payment had first been made to the agency. The client pays an initial 'lifetime enrolment fee' and buys a book of service forms. The service forms are sold in four sizes of books, 50, 100, 200, 400, price depending on quantity. When an account needs servicing, the client completes a service form and sends it to CPA. Customers are advised to use the service forms when any account is overdue by more than 14 days. On receipt of the form, CPA despatches a personally addressed letter to the debtor instructing him to settle his overdue account direct to the client. A cycle of personalized letters will be sent to the debtor until successful recovery.

As soon as payment has been received by the client, or the matter resolved in some other way, he tells CPA, using a special report card; he also tells the company what further action is needed. If the cash is not paid, the customer can instead ask CPA to sue on his behalf.

There is also a guarantee which provides that unless CPA recovers at least ten times the cost of the service fees are refunded. And in the case of an unsuccessful recovery a free substitute service form is provided.

One of the key features of the CPA service are the 'reminder' labels (see Figure 5.1) which are available free and in any quantity to members. These are fixed to invoices as they are raised and, according to CPA, 'have the effect of ensuring that the majority of your statements are brought to the top of the pile and paid to your terms'.

The CPA invoice stickers that tell the customer from square one that he will have trouble if he shirks timely payment must be a huge, intimidating plus point of the system. The firm boasts a 90 per cent success rate overall and 60 per cent payment response inside seven days. The service forms are valid for five years.

The pecuniary advantage, for the client, of having his debtor pay him and not his credit agency is clear. There is a less obvious psychological advantage —for the debtor (and, long term, for the creditor who continues to trade amicably). A debtor who, on prompting, pays up the money to a credit agency is a clearly documented late payer. The creditor firm knows he's a dog; the credit agency knows it; and, worth remembering, the debtor's bank manager may even note that a cheque has gone to a debt firm. With the CPA scheme, the dog isn't given a bad name. Where the debtor pays the client direct, the fact that he was prodded into action can be conveniently overlooked; it usually is. The debtor can convince himself that 'I was always going to pay up,' and, to prove it, he did. Only an uncouth credit sleuth could tell a different story.

How many times does a customer say to himself, 'So-and-so won't take us to court; he can't afford it,' or 'It wouldn't be worth his while'? To counter this, CPA introduced its 'Insured Invoice Plan'. It offers cover against legal costs of up to £1000 per claim when you have to sue for the recovery of money owed to you.

The insurance scheme is not only a form of civil defence but, as with the invoice stickers, should have a real deterrent effect once clients know a creditor is party to the CPA scheme.

CPA says: 'The total subscription per invoice is fixed, regardless of the amount invoiced. Currently this works out at around the cost of a postage stamp, with no percentages, no ledger fees, and no hidden costs. It is far less expensive than credit insurance or factoring.'

The United Association for the Protection of Trade Limited

The United Association for the Protection of Trade Ltd, better known as UAPT, began in 1842, when a group of businessmen got together to pool information about the creditworthiness of their customers. Today UAPT is one of the market leaders, still non-profitseeking, being run by an honorary committee of management drawn from membership, but operating services that benefit from a vast store—well over sixteen and a half million names on file—of credit information contained in its National Credit Register (NCR).

The NCR is a tool of consumer credit, primarily, and contains positive as well as adverse information about customers, records from official registries, county-court judgments, bills of sale, bankruptcies and the Scottish near-equivalents of the English legal processes; decrees, trust deeds and sequestrations. The emphasis is on quick, accurate information.

UAPT will give information while you wait, over the phone. Three names can be given at one time. (Phoning a *local* UAPT branch helps cut call costs.) Or give the names and addresses of a number of subjects and call back for the answers. Verbal information can be confirmed in writing, and telex is also available.

The benefit of working with a well-established company like UAPT is the fact that members feed in information about their customers and this is available to all—though a UAPT member cannot discover which fellow trader praised or blamed his own intended customer.

The Association also offers, through its commercial division, a complete range of reports on sole traders, partnerships and limited companies. Again the phone is used extensively. While you hold on, the Commercial Register will be searched for records of liquidations, receiverships, county court judgments, as well as member-supplied details of credit transactions, both successful and otherwise. A company profile adds to the above information photocopies of the latest accounts and directors' reports, details of capital structure, registered office, directors, shareholdings and charges. Other commercial reports, varying in intensity, and cost, are on tap. Debt collection is a further UAPT service.

The Central Register of UAPT has been brought 'on-line'; 5000000 Records are loaded on the newly commissioned Burroughs 6800 computers. From a UAPT member's point of view, this means that he now has the opportunity to access information directly from the Association's computer. The member's terminal will be a tele-type, which can be linked via an ordinary telephone. He will be able to communicate with the computer via the keyboard of the tele-type. To start a search, all he'll need to do is key in a user code and type out the name and address of the credit applicant. The printed reply will whizz back in seconds. A more sophisticated type of tele-type, with a memory, will enable use to be made of the cheap-period telephone rates. Association members with a very large volume of business could make use of a permanent link, possibly with a line printer, and use a VDU for all their information gathering and emitting processes.

Dr Brian Bailey, deputy director-general of UAPT, is on record as saying that sources of information like the traditional bank reference and creditor's previous experience may need to be re-examined in the light of new evidence. He decries the use of a bank reference because of the built-in delay, often as much as a week, he says. And relying on the creditor's previous experience with the customer also demands some rethinking. He mentions a study in America which revealed that it is often at the fourth or fifth renewed agreement that the customer defaults or 'goes bad.' In the UK, too, repeat customers who score the same as new customers can also have a higher default rate. He concludes that further checks from a credit-information agency must be a safer bet.

Inter-Credit International Limited

My contact with Inter-Credit International Ltd was not entirely academic. It was just before Christmas and I had just placed two consecutive advertisements in a Sunday newspaper. The paper reproduced the first advertisement precisely as ordered. But the second one did not appear. I was furious. The paper argued that yes, they had been at fault, they had forgotten to insert the ad, and therefore I was due to pay for just the one. It seemed perfectly straightforward—to them. But to me it was far more serious. The run-up period to Christmas is unique in the sales calendar. There is never as good an opportunity at any other time in the year. Further, advertisements of the sort I was placing, even over a period as short as two weeks, have a cumulative effect. So not placing the second ad was, to my mind, far more grave than just a 50 per cent success rate, and I told the paper so in no uncertain terms.

After some protracted correspondence—which must have cost that company at least as much as the amount outstanding—I received a short, sharp letter from Inter-Credit International Ltd. The note threatened legal proceedings if the money was not paid into their offices within 72 hours of receipt of the letter. And their closing sentence added a nice touch: 'First-class postage is advised.' The letter worked and I paid up; it had all been too much trouble.

Inter-Credit International call their debt collection by the milder term, Account Collection. Apparently I received their initial letter sent to me by my specially allocated co-ordinator, one of the unique features of their system. Had I not responded, the account would have immediately passed to the telephone collection department. There would have followed a series of follow-up calls until the account was settled. The co-ordinator handles day-to-day business with the client, answers all queries raised by a particular client's debtors, and he's also responsible for raising and completing the monthly report on all debts held by Inter-Credit for the client. The firm claims: 'This two-fold method has proven to result in far higher collections over a shorter period, at the same time ensuring that clients are kept fully informed of progress.... Most accounts are settled within two weeks due to this intensity of effort and the cash can be forwarded to the client daily.' Fees for this service are based on the age and number of accounts.

Inter-Credit also offer a status-reporting service, UK and overseas, on companies, firms, partnerships and all registered businesses. The claimed strengths of the system are (a) the ability to obtain current up-to-date trading information from suppliers (not the references given by the prospective customer); (b) non-reliance on purely historical financial information; and (c) supplying credit clearance information swiftly to the busy credit executive.

For their tracing service, Inter-Credit claim a 60 per cent success rate for individuals—'Individuals are more difficult to trace than firms'—and a 75 per cent success rate for firms and companies. In-depth tracing is also offered, and the success rate is currently 98 per cent.

On offer, too, is a comprehensive legal service with 'fixed fees, no pre-payments and the benefit of specialized legal advice on collection of overdue accounts'. Charges for a successful legal action are court disbursements, the company's normal commission (averaging 10 per cent, depending on age of the debt, nature of the debt, etc.), together with a fixed scale fee.

The firm has also recognized the attractive PR potential of educational services. Inter-Credit holds credit seminars, as well as offering credit consultancy. They also produce free helpful booklets, among them *Commercial Debt Collection*, *Legal Action in Collecting Accounts*, *Techniques of Account Collection*; and a highly recommended tele-prompter, a simple flip-open booklet, which is a programmed self-defence guide to all the different twists and turns a wriggling debtor will make over the phone.

Dun & Bradstreet Limited

Dun & Bradstreet are to the credit-agency business what Hoover are to vacuum cleaners. If clients take the great size ('the world's largest commercial credit-rating and debt-recovery organization') of D&B for granted, D&B certainly appear not to. The range of services offered, already staggering, is frequently added to and improved upon and—vital in this, as in many spheres—it is well publicized.

There is a UK and overseas credit-reporting/status-reporting service; a collection service with a network of 265 offices in 22 countries, with agents in 30 more countries; an export support service that pinpoints suitable trading outlets and vets them, before supplying a 'thoroughly researched list of contacts'.

The balance sheet service can include advice on interpretation, or expert, impartial comment. There is an external D&B study course in credit and financial analysis and a busy publishing division. D&B, owners of Stubbs Ltd, publish the famous *Stubbs Gazette*—it lists liquidations, bankruptcies, appointments of receivers, county court judgments or the equivalent for Scotland and Northern Ireland, mortgages and charges—*Who Owns Whom*, and numerous other authoritative reference books for the businessman. A recent addition to the publications portfolio is *D & B Creditnews*, a monthly newsletter for financial and credit managers.

The company operates an interesting unit system for payment. Each service carries a fee, charged in units. Thus a UK credit report costs 25 units. The commercial collection service for the UK costs 6 units for each placement, but a commercial collection request for an overseas subject costs 45 units for a placement, and both take commission charges on top. The units vary in cost according to a sliding scale, calibrated according to a customer's needs and budget.

When you begin to look through the literature, available free and in handfuls, from the various debt organizations, you may ask yourself leading questions. Such as: Why don't we, as a big company, set up our own collection operation, run from a separate address, with new staff (but answerable to and guided by the financial bosses at HQ), and, most important, using a completely different logo and letterhead style, to maintain the appearance of independence from the parent company, and borrow the known advantages of third-party intervention?

You would need to get a licence to trade as a collection agency and need to get your sums right; for setting up such an operation could prove costly.

Interdebt

Interdebt, the operating division of Granada Credit Collection Ltd, came up with a solution that cuts the corner off the cost problem. They produce collection letters, tastefully printed in black but with their name and the words 'FINAL NOTICE' forcefully added in red. The letters, available by the ream, are priced, on a sliding scale, according to quantity bought.

The customer first exhausts his own collection armoury, then sends the

Interdebt letter. He types in his own name in the 'CREDITOR' section and, above the name of the debtor, adds the latter's phone number, account/invoice number, amount overdue. The Interdebt letter carries the punchline '...failing receipt of payment within SEVEN DAYS, the creditor will receive our recommendations with a view to legal action in the Court...' A footnote states clearly: 'PAYMENT SHOULD BE MADE DIRECT TO THE CREDITOR...ANY COMMUNICATION SHOULD BE MADE IN WRITING.' Apparently, this last titbit is often ignored as debtors with the wind up, as well as those with grievances and queries, do in fact telephone Interdebt—which is no bad thing, as response is an important step and the creditor can quickly be brought into the picture.

The Interdebt letters have a top copy, sent to the debtor, a client copy, retained by the customer-creditor, and a bottom copy, the Account Progress Form, which is sent to Interdebt by the customer. Clearly the creditor must contact Interdebt fast once the money comes in or else the latter will start its dunning follow-up procedure.

Interdebt say: 'Experience has shown that a high percentage of debtors pay on receipt of the Interdebt "Final Notice" and no further action is required. You will have enjoyed all the benefits of third-party involvement for a few pence per form.'

Depending on the type of trade, and based on actual results, Interdebt claims a success rate of 65 to 95 per cent. An example shows true interest rate of collection costs as a percentage of cash cleared in the £0–£10000 domestic category. Assume an average invoice value of £50.

You would require 200 Interdebt letters @ 50p = £100.
The success rate of Interdebt ranges from 65–95 per cent.

Assuming a worst success rate, then:

65 % of £10000 = £6500 collected for £100 = 1.5 %.

Using the optional follow-up system, the balance of £3500 would be subject to a 10 % fee on a no collection—no fee basis. Again assuming a worst performance of 65 per cent:

65 % of £3500 = £2275 @ 10 % = £227.50

Therefore the overall success rate is 88 %, and the cost to the customer of collection £8775 = £327.50 representing a true rate of 3.7 %

Any remaining Doubting Thomases can try the Interdebt system against their own by taking up the company's trial offer of 20 letters.

Instead of the creditor having to ask for follow-up action, there is also an option of having Interdebt act, on your behalf, to chase debtors automatically.

Follow-up procedure begins after 10 days; there is an extra charge for this service, but no additional fee on successful collection. And no charge is billed until a transaction has been successfully completed.

Protea Management Service, an associated company, sells video and audio collecting aids: *Accounts collection by telephone*, a workbook and cassette package; and *Credit management—video programme.*

Sales Ledger Control Services Limited

Andrew Allies is the managing director of Sales Ledger Control Services, a bland sounding name that belies the forensic nature of Allies's skills and those of the consultants who work with him. He describes his speciality as 'the collection of UK debts', has worked for 120 companies in the last five years, and proudly name-drops—Ilford, Otis, Borg Warner. He employs five people of credit manager calibre who go out, on contract, to do collection work on site. Allies himself is frequently in the field, trouble-shooting or teaching (his first love), training staff in-house in telephone collection techniques, in which Allies is an acknowledged UK expert. 'The problem with letters is that there is a built-in delay cycle. Even a letter which reaches its target and is replied to almost immediately can take 10 days to turn around. So it takes 10 to 14 days to be sure your letter has been ignored. Two letter cycles would give your debtor five weeks' stolen credit.' The telephone, he believes, offers much tighter control, quicker response and greater flexibility.

Allies is frequently called on to comment, critically, on companies' collection procedures in the form of a report. In the course of his investigations he has perfected a number of interesting techniques, one of which—Comparative Percentage Analysis—he describes as 'the only diagnostic measurement of credit control success'.

He pinpoints problems with the traditional yardstick for credit control success, the DSO, days' sales outstanding. 'The calculation of DSO is at best a barometric measurement, telling you *generally* whether you have performed better or worse than last month/year. It gives no indication of which aspects of the collection activity are better or worse than desired.' Worrying overmuch about DSO, he says, leads to too great an emphasis on the paying behaviour of big customers, an understandable preoccupation, but one that glosses over the importance, in Allies's opinion, of smaller customers and their queries: 'As much as $\frac{2}{9}$ of the money owing to a firm has been known to be tied up in queries.'

Comparative Percentage Analysis offers a new way of working with an old tool, the aged debt schedule. One of the bonuses of the system is that it shows, at a glance, the pay progress of a month's accounts: how much of it has been cleared, as a percentage, within terms, within 31 to 60 days, within 61 to 90 days, and over. Clearly if the responsibility for collecting a single firm's accounts is passed, month to month, to a different collection officer and the progress monitored, this would offer a possible guideline for evaluating the success or otherwise of the different officers' collection techniques. Performance evaluation in the credit department is another of Allies's special areas of expertise.

Andrew Allies lectures regularly for The Institute of Credit Management on collection techniques.

The British Mercantile Group of Companies

The British Mercantile Group of Companies (BMG), formed in 1855, offers a wide selection of credit services for manufacturers and distributors in all trades and specializes in certain trades, among them paper and stationery, pharmaceuticals and toiletries, photographic, grocery, and more. The group offers: credit information on UK and overseas customers; overdue-account collection, with regular computer reporting and control; an in-house legal department; an export overdue-account collection; insolvency representation and reports; recruitment of credit staff; training in telephone collection techniques: consultancy on credit management; and news bulletins. This year the firm is expected to be fully computerized; the prospect of VDU client access to credit information, debt-chasing progress, etc., is round the corner.

An annual subscription is payable in advance. Thereafter, commission is charged on a sliding scale, according to the amount recovered. Where there is no recovery, no commission is charged. Recovered cash is paid into a clients' trust account and is passed to the customer, once a month, fully accounted, less the month's charges. All staff handling money are bonded by Fidelity Insurance.

BMG have staff in daily attendance at Companies House. Credit reports are available in three forms. The 'Standard' offers information from the BMG's up-to-date files of debts. As well as the debt history of the customer there will be suppliers' reports and local agents' reports.

The 'Express' report is recommended for clients who get a substantial order for immediate delivery. Time is at a premium, so the service guarantees an opinion in 72 hours. The 'Special' report is again for extra large orders and includes in-depth analysis of trading figures. Interim reports may also be issued to build up a complete and accurate trading picture.

Figure 7.1 How one company markets its friendly, but firm, collection procedure

The group offers no series of letters, but instead an immediate final letter. Member companies may have sent out up to six letters in their own collecting cycle, says managing director Don Jerome, before BMG will step in—'We look to be instructed when a debt is two to three months overdue.' He adds that the reasons that debtors respond to his firm's terse demand are:

1. They are a third party
2. They are a credit reporting agency
3. They have a special standing within the trade.

As the literature points out, 'The debtor will also realize—because of our reputation in the trade—that failure to pay the account may possibly damage his credit standing with other suppliers unless he pays promptly.'

The debtor is given no days' grace. In the letter sent out by The Paper Trade Protection Agency, a BMG member company, the demand reads: '...unless we receive settlement of the above account by return of post our clients will have no alternative but to instruct their solicitors to issue LEGAL PROCEEDINGS WITHOUT FURTHER NOTICE for recovery of the outstanding account....'

Mr Jerome has great faith in the effectiveness of telephone collection, and is associated with telephone expert, Andrew Allies, mentioned earlier. Don Jerome is convinced many companies would do better phoning than writing. After the 'final' group letter is sent out a phone call is made to check receipt of the letter (first-class post), to discover if there is still any unresolved query, and so on. Although the request is for payment by return and the final letter goes out first class, the phone call is not made for a week. For debts below £5000 a trained collection clerk calls, above that sum a collection manager takes command.

'The gist of the phone call,' says Don Jerome, 'is..."we have written to you to recover the amount outstanding...there has been no response...now we are taking clients' instructions...is there any chance that you are going to pay the outstanding amount to avoid the necessity for legal proceedings...?" This routine is adapted and improvised. In fact, some debtors are so close that they say: "Don't write to us—please phone"!'

Mr Jerome insists: 'We will accept every reasonable offer to pay.' Offers of part payment, instalments, queries are swiftly transmitted back to the creditor. 'There can be an adequate reason why a debt hasn't been paid. It's important to obtain the reason to maintain goodwill; you can build on goodwill. The human element is vital. It's no good going in feet first; a problem should be discussed.' It is vital, he says, for a client to keep in close contact.

Companies who subscribe to BMG are generally turning over in excess of

£100 000 and often much more. One-off debt-collection shots are undertaken, though never lightly. Payment, requested in advance, includes a percentage of the debt itself and a fee for collection. A letter of authority instructing BMG to undertake collection of the debt must accompany a written request—verbal solicitations are not enough.

8. Bringing in the law

When should you sue? Rarely, is the short answer. The fact of having to should be shaming—for you. If something goes wrong with your collection programme, directly or indirectly, you are to blame. All of the following faults may be indicated: your assessment data are too skimpy; your assessment data are incorrectly interpreted; your assessment data are correctly interpreted but you nevertheless make the wrong decision (a customer has promise but is just starting up, for instance, and you decide to overrule the indications that trade is inadvisable); you ignore the 'Indian signs' of pending trouble along the payment route; your collection programme is lacking; your collection agency is at fault.

There may be other, more subtle, factors working against you, however. You may, for instance, have made all the right moves, but although you acted appropriately you were not taken seriously. This does not mean threatening legal action at every turn; quite the opposite: never make any threat unless you intend to carry it out. A customer who gets wind that you make idle threats will become a Nobel-prize-winning liberty taker. And when you do threaten legal action, follow it up swiftly.

But first make sure your threat is understood and clearly documented. One collection firm states: "...unless this amount is received at these offices within 72 hours of receipt of this letter, legal proceedings will be instituted....' Knowing the post, there could be a delay of anything up to 10 days between sending a letter and its arrival. Together with the three days' grace offered to the recipient, that's another fortnight's stolen credit. Presumably the grace period *after arrival* is to give the letter all the time in the world to arrive and the debtor no excuse for non-payment, by first-class post, once it *has* arrived. But why not send the 'legal' letter by first-class recorded delivery, state that it is 'RECORDED DELIVERY' on the letter, and demand payment within seven days of the postmark? That way the opening and closing date of the dunning cycle are clear and irrefutable. And if there is any untoward delay, such as a postal strike, there is always the phone number, with the onus on the lazy payer to pull his finger out and use it.

Some firms send letters designed to put the wind up their debtors by using a feint combined with quasi-legal jargon: 'If we do not hear from you within a week you will be deemed to have admitted liability.' It doesn't really help, though it might spur action, because merely ignoring allegations is not, in law, the same thing as admitting them.

It is more important to be able to prove your debt, by means of letters of contract, invoices, statements, etc. An invoice is sometimes the only bit of evidence submitted by firms that regularly and successfully dun clients through the courts.

Take time, now, to look at the sort of information a solicitor needs before he'll lift a finger to send a dunning letter or threaten legal action. Then, next time, work backwards; make sure your own records are meticulously kept, just in case. Your cheapest insurance policy against bad debts is your own careful vetting of clients and painstaking documentation. In business it pays to hope for the best—but always to be prepared for the worst.

A solicitor's checklist of information includes:

- Creditor's full name, address and title or trading style.
- Address of registered office if a limited company.
- Registration number.
- Whether the debt is due to the client or to a subsidiary, a director in person, to the client's wife; similarly for the debtor—is he liable personally?
- Size of original balance, balance outstanding, nature of business. Most transactions involve goods sold, services rendered or work done and materials provided. The solicitor needs to know which.
- When the debt first became due.
- How long to offer the debtor to pay up—three days or a week being typical —in the preliminary letter.
- Confirmation that the amount owing is undisputed.
- Unequivocal instructions for him to be able to accept payment by instalments if offered or to proceed directly to court if the cash is not paid. A solicitor also works better when he knows something about the commitments of the debtor; he then knows what the latter can afford.
- The solicitor must know the small print of your deal because there is always the chance that the debtor will phone him. Be sure to enclose all the copy invoices and check that they add up to the total outstanding. A tiny detail may be all that stands in the way of return-of-post payment; folly indeed for the solicitor to have to keep the hot and responsive debtor on ice while he chases you for information which should be to hand.

What should spark legal action?

You don't sue to make good a 'bad debt'. Bad debts are uncollectable debts; they're the ones you claim VAT and tax relief on. The debtor who needs the legal treatment is just a very bad payer. Some firms sue as a matter of course, after a certain point is passed in their collection programme. They do it *pour encourager les autres*, as the Foreign Legion might shoot stragglers on a 50-mile Sahara hike, just to help the others find their second wind. You probably cannot afford that kind of luxury, not that suing is necessarily expensive, but because it can be time-consuming and in small businesses, where the proprietor is closely involved with day-to-day running of accounts, it disrupts the flow of business, and that is bad news at any price.

'Triggers' of legal action are almost universally accepted by businessmen. Legal action is called for, it is agreed, where there is no response to letters, the debtor is habitually unavailable on the phone, a cheque bounces, the debtor avoids your salesman, there are disturbing rumours about pending insolvency and you feel you had better get in quick before another creditor does and scoops whatever little cash remains.

The 'no response' trigger points to two vital ingredients that should be present in every collection routine. The first is that opportunity should be given at just about every stage for the debtor to voice a query. There may be a genuine grievance, such as non-delivery of goods, dissatisfaction, non-allowance of an agreed credit on goods, failure to comply with a customer's invoicing demands ('send two copies' or 'send invoice to our head office in Leeds'), and so on. Close to a quarter of a firm's receivables may be tied up in unresolved queries, asserts one credit consultant. The usual prompt is along the lines: 'If there is any reason why payment has not been made, please telephone. . . on. . . without delay.'

The other ingredient spotlighted is the need to telephone as well as write. A one-man business cannot reply to letters if that man is out of the country. A phone call will quickly tell you he's not there. Likewise, there may be any number of reasons why a letter has not been replied to, such as non-delivery of your missive (rare, but not unknown). A phone call clears it up. You'll know pretty smartly from phone calls, when you leave a number and the call is not returned, that you are being cold-shouldered.

Just before going to law consider the halfway house remedy of sending a solicitor's letter. A lawyer shaping up for action, on paper, is a pretty awe-inspiring sight. A legal letter implies eventual suit, and this may have the purgative effect that a suite of dunning letters and a barrage of phone calls fail to have.

A further reason to consider this course is that you can take advantage of your session with the solicitor to talk over your grievance, just to be sure you have a cast-iron case before proceeding to court. Free, helpful information is available from the legal expert at your local Citizens' Advice Bureau (CAB), or the Legal Advice Centre nearest to you. You have to be pretty poor to get legal aid these days, but many solicitors are party to the legal aid scheme, which often means you can chat to one for 30 minutes for a fiver; your CAB will tell you who your £5 lawyers are.

Who should handle your case?

Could you 'sue-it-yourself'? Many have, successfully, and these days it's easier than ever to handle your own case in the county court. Or you could use a solicitor or hire the services of a collection agency's solicitor. The latter, with his vast experience of debt cases, will be adept at cutting the legal cackle. But the amount of money owing may dictate your best bet—especially with astronomic solicitors' fees.

If the amount owing is £500 or less, you can sue in the local county court with the minimum of formality and cost as the claim will go to arbitration. The county court can deal with claims of up to £5000, and you can institute or defend your own case, as in any civil court. But your opponent will, likely as not, be professionally defended and mistakes would be costly: they could lead to an astronomical bill if you lose—that of the defendant's legal costs.

When a claim is heard by arbitration no solicitor's charges are recoverable, though court costs—the summons and enforcement of an award, if needed—and costs that the arbitrator considers to be incurred through the unreasonable conduct of the defendant are reimbursed. Fees paid to an expert witness and the cost of travel are also recoverable.

Until 21 April 1981 the informal arbitration procedure in the small claims court was not automatic; it had to be asked for. No wonder some plaintiffs were surprised when they were faced with full court hearing. But now claims for less than £500 are automatically dealt with by arbitration, unless the registrar agrees to order a court trial. He will be guided by questions such as: Does a case involve a difficult point of law or fact? Is fraud involved? Do both parties want the trial to go to court?

For small claims, the court is just a room, not the court auditorium, and the parties sit round a table. To emphasize the lack of formality, the Registrar, the usual arbitrator, sheds his gown. Both sides are encouraged to be their own advocates and can produce evidence and call witnesses. The other very good reason for not hiring a professional is that even if you win your case you will rarely be awarded legal expenses and the court costs are low. The cost of issuing a summons is '10p for every £1 or part thereof claimed', with a minimum fee of £4. If a bailiff serves your summons (you can do it yourself), that's also £4. There are several handy, simple-language guides available to help you handle your own case, among them *How to Sue*, from the Consumers' Association, Caxton Hill, Hertford, and the free publication, *Small Claims in the County Court*, published by the Lord Chancellor's office, and available from county courts.

At this point, a word of warning gleaned from the *Small Claims* booklet. Its principal purpose, it says, is to tell you how to sue in the county court. Whether it is worth your while to do so is another matter. Little satisfaction is gained from winning an action if your opponent has no money to pay the judgment debt.

Another noteworthy element for a successful outcome is whether you have given the other party sufficient opportunity to consider your claim and come to an amicable settlement. The courts like to see people given a fair chance. But I take it for granted that if you've got this far in the book, suing is the last of the many positive steps you have already taken.

Whom do you sue?

The court serves the summons on the defendant, but it's not up to them to check names and addresses. You must be sure you sue the right person at the right place.

You may think you know where your client lives, his correct trading style, name of the proprietor, and so on. But do you? A 'sell! sell! sell!' policy can result in blind enthusiasm, effectively whiting out what should be the normal careful practice of verifying basic details and making sure every transaction is not only fully documented, with copies in your own file, but is, as far as possible, independently certified—communications sent recorded delivery or by registered post.

Don Jerome, managing director of the British Mercantile Group of Companies, tells of one publisher client who was fretting over payment long overdue for some books sent to India. 'We investigated and discovered that the books had been sent to an address that was the fourth tree in the third row in a park in Delhi! Not only that, but they were sent by parcel post and the debtor denied receiving them!'

Do you know the first name or full initials of all the people you trade with? A private individual should be sued in his own name; surname and initials will do at a pinch with the word 'male,' in brackets, to follow. A woman must be described as a 'widow,' 'spinster' or 'femme sole'—divorcee.

A partnership can be sued in the name of the firm, for when one partner enters into a contract all the partners are jointly liable. It's a mistake to single out a single partner—even if he is the troublemaker—as even having won your case, if he cannot pay, you will not be allowed to sue the other partners. On paper the description should read either 'Mel Lewis & Co (a firm),' or, with a two-partner firm, 'Mel Lewis & Lem Siwel trading as Mel Lewis & Co (a firm).'

A sole proprietor can be sued under his own name or in the name of his business. A summons can be served on individuals at their home address or place of business. Reference books at a local library (electoral roll) or at council offices (rate books) will help you locate and name fully the person you're after. Full particulars of a Limited Company will be found at the Companies Registration Office—London Search Room, Companies House, 55–71 City Road, London EC1Y 1BB. But remember it is the 'registered office' of the company to which the summons must be sent—and that may be a different address from the shop, office or factory you have been dealing with. (PS: why not get the registered address in future when opening an account?)

Normally the court bailiff delivers the summons in person, but you can do it yourself, and may have to if the court cannot locate your quarry. When you find him you may have trouble getting him to actually grasp the nettle of his impending discomfiture. If so, just throw the summons on the ground in front of him, like the proverbial gauntlet. If the proprietor, partner or director is not available—and you have made a good effort to contact him—a summons can be handed to anyone who *appears* to be running the business. A written notice must accompany the summons. It states: 'Take notice that this summons is served on you as the person having apparent control of...,' naming the firm or company. A summons can be posted if you are sure the debtor will be aware of its presence within twelve days of delivery. But unless you are dealing with a limited company at its official address, it is wiser to get the thing delivered by hand by the bailiff or do it yourself.

The Clerk at the county court cannot advise you on the tricky points of suing, such as whether you have a worthwhile case. But he will help with the nitty gritty, like filling in the Request Form, to get the ball rolling, the Particulars of Claim Form, which type of summons is appropriate to your case, and so on. Most debt cases involve a default summons; an ordinary summons is issued when the sum in question is not clear, e.g., a claim for personal injury in a road accident.

Choose the right court first time and save time

A local court will tell you which is the right court to choose for your action; you'll find a list in the telephone directory under 'Courts'. Usually this will be either the court for the district in which your debtor lives or works, or the court that covers the area in which the debt was incurred. Contracts made by post are slightly more finicky. If you order goods by mail order and send the money in an envelope, the contract is made when you post the letter, i.e., in your neighbourhood. But if you write to order goods the contract is made when the order is accepted, i.e., at the premises of the firm. Even if you make a mistake about the court, actions can be transferred without a lot of fuss, just loss of valuable time.

Once you have filled in the Request Form, supplied by the court with the Particulars of Claim, and paid the fee, the court gets on with preparing the summons. Meanwhile they issue you with a plaint note which does double duty as a receipt for your fee and a reference for your forthcoming action. The plaint number must always be mentioned in any correspondence, as court records are filed by numbers, not names. And on any trip to court remember to take with you your plaint note.

Quite often by the time the debtor has got wind of an upcoming court action he will be beating a path to your door to give you the money and spare the hassle. Or he may just sit tight, fully intending to pay up when he must, but happy effortlessly to make more capital out of your funds while he waits for the court to find in your favour. In such circumstances winning the decision is almost automatic. If the defendant doesn't pay up, deliver an admission or a defence or a counterclaim within 14 days of being served with the summons, you can have judgment entered, using a form obtainable from the court. You'll need to show your plaint note at this point, but it can be done by post provided you enclose an s.a.e.

You can ask for all of the debt to be paid in a lump sum. But if you know this will break the back of the debtor and he'll give you a further runaround for your money, you can ask for the pay-off to be in instalments. The villain can also admit his liability (a form of admission, defence and counterclaim comes with the summons) and opt for time to pay. But if you don't like the size of his proposed payments or their proposed frequency, a meeting can be arranged (a 'disposal') at which you can do your Perry Mason act and ask pertinent probing questions about the debtor's income, produce evidence of his Bahamian bank account, and suchlike. However, it may pay you in the long run to accept payments smaller than you would wish because the easier payment is made, the more likely are you to get paid.

Incidentally, never pull back from court proceedings just because the debtor comes up with an enticing instalment plan. Get a judgment first. Then, if the debtor defaults on his payments you can enforce the judgment, and there is no need to go through the legal process again.

You've got your judgment, but you still haven't got the money

Because getting paid is the name of this game, and even at this stage of play you may be trumped by a fly debtor, it's as well to know what to do if the money promised, in whole or in parts, is not forthcoming.

Written advice is available, in the form of the free county-court publication *Enforcing Money Judgments in The County Court*. It will help you extract money from a debtor provided he has some. If a county-court judgment remains unsatisfied for more than 28 days, it is registered in the Unsatisfied County Court Judgment Register, which is open to public inspection. Clearly this could affect a debtor's credit ratings.

The first and most commonly used remedy is a Warrant of Execution. The court bailiff is ordered, by the court, to go to the premises of the defendant, select suitable goods and sell them with a view to realizing the amount owed. The actual seizure is preceded by a warning note which can result in the more saleable items—colour telly, music centres, antiques—going on a short holiday before the bailiff arrives. Another ploy is to claim that goods are the subject of a hire-purchase agreement or 'they belong to my wife/husband'. In a High Court case, a Writ of Execution is the equivalent licence to purloin private property, and here it is the Sheriff of the County who wades in. Sheriffs have a better track record, it seems, for coming away with the goods; possibly because Sheriffs work on a commission basis, while bailiffs are salaried.

A garnishee order could provide an unexpected dream topping

Garnishee procedure is a side-stepping ploy that is not given adequate attention by business people turned into reluctant and occasional debt collectors by their sticky-fingered clients. Suppose you discover that Mr X owes your debtor some money, you can apply to the court, on affidavit, for the issue of a summons to be served on Mr X. A hearing is held and if Mr X admits he owes the money he may have to pay it to you and not to the debtor. Not much chance of finding a Mr X? Perhaps not. But it is possible to garnishee a debtor's bank account. The best time to 'raid' that of a salaried person is the last Thursday in the month. So it makes sense, with consumer business to ask a new credit customer whether he is paid by cheque and even when. Interested now?

If Mr Y is on PAYE you can Pinch As Y Earns

An employed individual (not self-employed) can be made the subject of an attachment of earnings order. Our Mr Y appears in court and is questioned about his work, earnings, commitments. An amount may then be deducted from his wage packet, and it is up to the employer to see that the court gets the money in order to pass it to the creditor. If the debtor changes jobs the employer must tell the court. But tracking down an itinerant professional debtor is easier said than done.

Bankruptcy, winding up, liquidation, fraudulent preference and fraudulent trading

The Registrar can issue a bankruptcy notice giving the defendant a week to pay the debt and costs. If he doesn't pay he will have committed one of the several 'acts of bankruptcy'. The beauty of the bankruptcy notice receiving order is that it will put the wind up an individual who is a company director because an undischarged bankrupt is not allowed to hold a directorship (or receive credit for more than £50, plus sundry other joy-killing vetoes). The procedure can be expensive and the debt must be over £200.

If judgment is given against a limited company and that company does not pay up, then the creditor may be able to file a petition for the compulsory winding up of the company. If the amount owing is more than £200 a company can be petitioned with only 21 days' notice, and judgment does not even need to be obtained. However, without first obtaining judgment the court is likely to throw out your petition. Nevertheless, as a frightener tactic it can be effective and result in payment where much else failed.

Connected with winding up are the tricky topics of fraudulent preference and fraudulent trading.

When a company's liabilities exceed its assets it instantly becomes, technically and legally at least, insolvent and must stop trading. In practice, many companies don't stop and they get away with it because the big pay-off is just round the corner—*they* get paid money owing to them—or because over a period they pull round and it's a relatively simple matter to juggle figures so that not even an accountant can spot that the company was up shoe creek at any point in the tax year.

Although in law an insolvent company must shut up shop, what often happens is that the money coming in is used to pay off the most pressing creditors, or those that carry the biggest threat. If a bank has taken a second mortgage on a director's house then quite likely the bank will continue to get paid on time and in full where other creditors of lesser standing get thrown a bone in part payment or, more likely, nothing at all.

If you, as one of the bone-picking creditors, get wind that this sort of preferential skulduggery is going on, then a threat to shop the company for fraudulent trading and fraudulent preference may work wonders for your own claim.

But what if *you* want some preferential treatment?

When you go to a bank for a loan, the bank manager will almost certainly want some security for his money. Like as not, he'll take a charge on something you own, often, as a private individual, it will be your most valuable possession, your home. Likewise, it is not unknown for creditors to take a charge on the assets of those with whom they are trading. And a charge is sometimes taken, late in the day, when a debtor cannot settle his account but wants to keep faith. Now if a liquidator is appointed less than a year after your charge is taken and the debtor pays you off, rather than forfeit his house or whatever, then he can be accused of fraudulent preference.

Paying off favoured creditors while knowingly insolvent carries stiff penalties. Under the 1980 Companies Act fraudulent trading carries a prison sentence of seven years' maximum or a fine without limit. As a creditor you may choose to take a chance and accept what may turn out to be a case of fraudulent preference. The worst thing that can happen is that you will have to pay back the money into the kitty which is divided up among all the insolvent company's creditors.

But there is a chance that the liquidator will be slow in getting round to you. Or the debtor may continue to trade for more than 12 months after the liquidator enters the scene, in which case your charge stands and the fraudulent preference tag will not apply.

Another very good reason for strongly *demanding* preferential treatment is that in the case of an eventual claim of fraudulent preference your diligence could count in your favour. For if you twisted your debtor's arm to make him pay you, then clearly he didn't 'prefer' to pay you. Besides which, it is up to the liquidator to show that there was *intent* to prefer you.

9. Insuring yourself against bad debts

Credit insurance

The best 'natural' insurance against damage from bad debts is, of course, to spread the debt load—and risk—over a large number of customers. In theory, no company should have any one debt so large that it could not survive the debtor's failure. But business life isn't so pat, and professional help may be needed. Paid-for credit insurance offers cover up to an agreed percentage of the debts insured, at a cost of a quarter to one per cent, as a rule. The question then becomes, is it cheaper, on an annual basis, to stomach bad debts than to pay to cover them?

The traditional argument for credit insurance goes like this. As a businessman you surely insure your place of work and equipment against loss or damage? Therefore how can you not insure what is probably your most valuable asset, your debtors, against 'loss or damage'—insolvency?

The answer may be blowing in the ill wind of change brought about by the recession. Debtors who might once have been solid are now at risk: 1980 was the liveliest year on record for business insolvencies. Credit insurance may become a necessity, rather than a tax-deductible luxury, but in becoming so, premiums are likely to increase to meet the greater risk of an accident-prone trading world.

Credit insurers insist that the insured submits the whole of his client list, not just a selection, presumably of the more risky ones; the clients' names, together with suggested credit limits, are submitted to the insurer who reserves the right to agree or reject not only the limits but also the names (the insurer may agree, for reasons of practicality, to stand for a customer's loss to the level of his credit rating in one of the standard credit-reference books, such as Dun & Bradstreet's Register).

Insurers who are likely to be serving several clients in the same industry, and with the same customers, are uniquely placed to cross-reference customer creditworthiness. If an insurer refuses to cover a company, there is probably a very good reason for it and one that should not be lost on the credit manager. Indeed the 'piggy in the middle' function of the credit insurer should be welcomed rather than not. To maintain the metaphor of the opening paragraphs, the factory that is an obvious fire risk will be refused cover until it has been brought up to scratch and made safer. Similarly, the insurer forces insured companies to trade with customers who are a better bet, so the whole level of risk is improved. Nor is it likely that an insured company will relax credit control because it is covered. On the contrary, a claim may be rejected if there is evidence that the debt has gone bad through slackness in collection procedure. So again, the insured company is encouraged to run a tighter ship.

Trade credit insurance, which is dominated by two mammoth companies, Trade Indemnity Co. Ltd and Credit & Guarantee Insurance Co. Ltd, earned itself something of an enviable reputation following the collapse of Rolls-Royce in 1971. When the Receiver was brought in, on February 4, one engineering firm had Rolls-Royce as a debtor to the tune of over £1 000 000. Proof of loss was passed to the insurance company on March 18 and four days later a settlement cheque arrived. Interesting to note here that Rolls-Royce had less than a Rolls-Royce reputation for paying their own debts on time. Where they were efficiently chased, so the records show, they would pay up in three to four months; otherwise they would hold out for eight to nine months. No wonder so many were left holding the baby!

Factoring

To some businesses a factoring service is a purchasable dream. The factor 'takes the waiting out of wanting' (apologies to Access card), by buying a company's debts and making quickly available the cash tied up in its accounts receivable. In a full factoring service the factor effectively takes over the factored client's sales-ledger accounting system and collects the debts; cash advances of up to 80 per cent of a firm's invoices are made on an agreed date each month, and the balance is paid when the cash comes in from the customer. The factor also offers insurance cover on bad debts, on recognized accounts to a pre-agreed credit limit of up to 100 per cent. Factors will generally not act for a company whose turnover is less than £100 000 (a £50 000 customer, however, may still find a taker and the trend seems to be a downward one), and will insist that individual invoices are for £100 plus.

As much as a factor will look carefully into the viability of a potential new client, studying its trading history, profitability, liquidity, capital, risk, number of creditors, and so on, so it will make good business sense to do your own market research into a prospective factoring company (a list of the eight main factors and their shareholders is given in Figure 9.1), comparing prices and

	%	*Shareholders*
Alex Lawrie Factors Ltd	75 25	Lloyds & Scottish First National Bank of Boston
Arbuthnot Factors Ltd	66⅔ 33⅓	Arbuthnot Latham Yorkshire Bank
Barclays Factoring Ltd	100	Barclays Bank Ltd
Credit Factoring International Ltd	100	National Westminster
Griffin Factors Ltd	100	Midland Bank Finance Corporation
H & H Factors Ltd	Majority—	Walter E Heller Overseas Corporation
Independent Factors Ltd	75 25	Lloyds & Scottish First National Bank of Boston
International Factors Ltd	75 25	Lloyds & Scottish First National Bank of Boston

Figure 9.1 Main UK factors and their shareholders

services (a minimum agreement period of one year with a three-month cancellation clause may be imposed by the factor). Also remember that the service elements offered by a factor—credit insurance, invoice discounting, sales-ledger control, debt collecting—may be available individually from other sources. Two typical disadvantages of sidestepping the factor's full service are: that with a simple invoice discounting the customer is still liable to make good any losses caused by insolvency, and credit insurance typically offers 75 to 90 per cent cover, set against the 100 per cent offered by a factor.

The full factoring service is usually 'disclosed'—the customer pays the factor, not the supplier. This has aroused suspicion in the past, when it was assumed, often wrongly, that a supplier was in financial trouble. Now, with the major UK banks heavily involved in factoring, this is unlikely to be an anxiety. Flexibility is also one of the advantages offered by the factor. With an invoice-discounting agreement, the client maintains his own sales ledger, collects his own debts, yet still enjoys the benefit of credit insurance. The cheques can be paid into a special disguised account; the service here is said to be 'undisclosed'. The insurance element alone may be enjoyed. The invoice-discounting agreement is said to be a 'without recourse' agreement, i.e., the supplier is insured against the failure of his customers; in a 'with recourse' agreement, he stands fully responsible for customers' insolvency, and will be obliged to make good any losses.

The traditional source of finance, the bank, which takes a 'past performance' view of the company's potential profitability, may be less suitable than a factor for a firm that is expanding fast, is exporting extensively (some factors have special export facilities), and is experiencing acute cash-flow problems as a kind of growing pain. A bank overdraft is, however, frequently cheaper than a factor's advance.

Among the biggest factors is Alex Lawrie, owned by Lloyds & Scottish and the First National Bank of Boston. Here's how Alex Lawrie explain their services and charges:

> You send all your invoices to us (in duplicate) as and when you raise them, or whenever you like. We send the top copy to your customer, who pays us directly.
>
> The day after receiving your invoices we send you an agreed amount, which can be up to 80 per cent of their value, less our service fee of between one-half and three per cent (both the agreed amount and the service fee are arranged in advance).
>
> The balance of the invoice value is paid to you as soon as your customer pays us. (You decide how much we chase them.) It is at this stage that we deduct the interest charge on the money we have provided... The rate we charge is $2\frac{1}{2}$ per cent over the Finance Houses Association rate which is reported daily in most quality newspapers. We think you will find that this is very much in line with what you are paying for your overdraft facility. In some cases less.
>
> We apply this rate on a day-to-day basis to the amount we paid you against an invoice. It is applied until the day that the invoice is paid to us by your customer.

The prospective client is then told the advantages of being factored, and is reminded: 'You cannot collect and sell at the same time. You sell—we collect.' Some firms, larger ones especially, with a well established and efficient sales ledger and collections department, do manage to do both perfectly well. Small firms—within the financial guidelines already mentioned—and medium-size companies are more likely to benefit from the services of a factor. The advantages, some easier to quantify than others, include saving of valuable management time—the boss is invariably called in when a debt passes beyond the written reminder or telephone collection stage—saving in staff salaries, office space, office equipment, stationery, post and other costs, when a factor takes over the sales-ledger accounting function. Incidentally, factors are likely to be more efficient at accounting and collection procedures, and are likely to use sophisticated computer systems probably far in advance of the methods used by the company considering using a factor's services.

The factor will be able to offer regular management reports, and these again will be of great help in decision-making and planning. The factored firm benefits from improved cash flow in several ways. Its own credit rating may be enhanced, once it is able to pay its own bills on time; the cash in hand can be used to take advantage of early payment discount offers; expansion and aquisition will be within easier reach. The debit side of the coin features two imponderables. What if the supplier's customers are upset by the new super-efficient collection system; if they are, does it matter? Those who are disturbed may be precisely the sort of customers who take discounts out of terms, delay payments for as long as possible; they may be well lost. The possibility that a factor's charges will increase is of some concern, because of the likelihood of a minimum contract period and the notice clause; resurrecting the former in-house sales-ledger accounting system may prove to be a tricky turnabout, although all the evidence shows that factored companies generally stay with their factors. Certainly the competition element will help keep factoring charges down. Factoring is more widely practised in the United States—where cash in hand, rather than full order books and fat invoices, is preferred—but is growing apace in the UK since the recession took hold in the late 1970s, and there is every sign that this pattern will continue.

Exporting

Exporting, one of the most specialized—and problem-fraught—areas of trade, is well covered in the specialist publications listed on pages 121–125. It is worth mentioning here, though, that expert help is available from the Government through the Export Credits Guarantee Department (ECGD). ECGD is the major source of credit insurance used by UK exporters. Default, insolvency and political risks are covered. Goods are usually insured from the date of shipment, but, for a higher premium, a 'contracts policy' offers cover from the date of contract. This is especially useful for firms that make bespoke goods, which take time to produce, leaving open the possibility that the customer fails even before shipment. Cover is offered (in both cases) subject to satisfactory credit reports. The rates are similar to those charged by credit insurers in the UK for the home market.

10. How to make the most of your unpaid bills

When VAT first became payable in the UK, in 1973, the official General Guide to VAT stated flatly: 'VAT cannot be waived on a taxable supply on the ground that the taxable person has not received the due payment from his customer, whatever steps he may have taken to recover the debt.'

Then in 1978 the rules were changed. VAT leaflet No. 8/78/VAC stated:

> As part of his Budget statement the Chancellor of the Exchequer announced that he was going to provide relief for the VAT lost by a registered trader when a debtor became formally insolvent. This change has now been approved by Parliament and comes into operation in respect of amounts owed by debtors who became formally insolvent. . . after 1 October 1978.

The Customs & Excise definition of a formal insolvency is precise: the debtor must have been adjudged bankrupt (i.e., there is an Order of Adjudication against him) or the court must have made an order for the administration in bankruptcy of his estate. Alternatively, 'if the debtor is a company, it must have become the subject of a creditors' voluntary winding up (insolvency commences when the winding up resolution is passed), or the court must have made an order for the company to be wound up.' Then the supplier needs to lodge a claim in the insolvency for the amount of the debt minus the VAT. He will claim the VAT element from Customs & Excise on his VAT return form (VAT 100). This assumes that the supplier has already paid to Customs & Excise the VAT he is claiming as bad-debt relief. Further conditions of entitlement include the stipulation that the supply was made for a consideration in money, and that ownership has passed to the customer. Relief cannot be claimed by a factor or anyone else to whom a debt has been sold. Nor, say Customs & Excise, can relief be claimed if the goods have been supplied under a contract

> 'containing a clause which reserves title in the goods to the supplier until such time as full payment has been received—unless the title in the goods has been formally passed to the liquidator/trustee as agent of the insolvent customer.'

But if you have insured yourself for the tax-inclusive amount of the debt this does not disqualify you from claiming relief. Further details of how to claim, and the various modifications that apply for Scottish bankruptcies are contained in leaflet No. 8/78/VAC.

How to play the VAT game—and win

VAT is due quarterly, with a month's grace period in which to make up accounts and finally pay. The VAT-registered trader makes out his invoice, adds on VAT, and sends it to the customer. Because of slow payment, and the nature of VAT returns, there is a reasonable chance that the trader has to find the VAT element to pay the Customs & Excise out of his own pocket—before he has been paid by his customer.

It works like this. If a quarter ends on February 28, the trader has until March 31 to complete his VAT form and pay the VAT bill (or possibly claim his VAT refund, if his entitlement to VAT relief exceeds his liability to pay VAT). That quarter would have begun on December 1.

Suppose the trader invoiced a customer for £115 (£100 plus 15 per cent VAT) on December 1. He would be obliged to pass across the £15 'VAT element' to the Government by March 31. Unless he runs a very sloppy ship, the trader would expect to have been paid by his customer before that date, four months further on, so would actually have the £15 in hand to pay. Clearly the closer the trader can get paid to December 1 the better, for then he has the use of the VAT money as long as possible. And VAT can easily amount to £1500 or £15000 in certain businesses: very useful sums indeed to have handy, and yet another reason to push for fast payment.

But what if the trader makes out an invoice on February 27—one day before the close of that VAT quarter? He still has to find £15 by March 31. And probably he won't have been paid by then. In fact, a trader has a minimum of one month, a maximum of four months to recoup VAT, which averages out at two and a half months. Eighty-day bills are on the slow side and relatively rare even by bad British standards, so it's not an unfair demand on the part of Customs & Excise.

However, shrewd businessmen will begin to see how they may actually benefit to the maximum from the VAT dating system by invoicing as close to the beginning of a VAT period as possible*—and then insisting on rapid payment!

* The procedure suggested above, say Customs & Excise, will be effective provided: (a) the invoices issued are tax invoices which contain the information specified in para. 38 of HM Customs & Excise notice 700, 'Value Added Tax: General Guide', revised Oct. 1979; (b) the date of issue of the tax invoice is the taxpoint for the suppliers invoiced under the rules set out in para. 14 of the notices.

Tax relief

In all the thousands of words written on tax, there is relatively little devoted to debts; from the point of view of this study, the most interesting points are raised in Sections 130 and 136 of the Taxes Act. Deduction for bad debts can be claimed if the debts can be proved to be such, and deduction for 'doubtful debts' can also be claimed, 'to the extent to which they are estimated as bad'.

A genuine bad trading debt can be claimed as an allowable expense in arriving at taxable profits. If your profit was £1000 and you had a bad debt of £100 you would pay tax on £900. The taxman appears to take a reasonable and practical view of bad debts; you would merely be required, in an examination of your accounts, to show evidence that the debt was bad—all the usual dunning documentation, copy invoices, statements, letter carbons (preferably with attached recorded delivery receipts), and so on.

A doubtful debt requires rather more of an act of faith on behalf of the taxman, and some inspired guesswork—not to mention honesty—on behalf of the creditor. He is asked to estimate how much of a debt is ever likely to be recovered. On a debt of £100 the creditor might conclude that he would eventually pull in £60. One hundred pounds is reflected in trading receipts in the normal way, but £40 is shown in the expenses column as a provision for doubtful debts. In a bankruptcy or a winding up, the creditor has to estimate the likely amount of dividend and similarly deduct the irrecoverable part of the debt.

You'll notice that the taxman, unlike the VATman, does not insist that a debtor be insolvent before allowing relief to his creditors. Nor does he insist that a supplier ceases to trade with a debtor for a debt to become claimable. If it could be shown that the debtor was experiencing a temporary setback and that you, as creditor, had every confidence in his recovery, then continuing to trade, in the taxman's view, would be understandable and acceptable business practice. One can begin to see, though, that this 'confidence in recovery' might need to be given concrete form in the amount shown in your balance sheet as estimated to be recovered!

11. How others made them pay

Getting your teeth into a debtor

I had a long chat about debtors with my dentist a while ago—if I have to pay for a half-hour of his time I feel justified in picking his brains for the rest of the time left over after he's been picking my teeth! It turned out that he knows all about getting teeth out of patients but nothing at all about extracting cash from them. 'I walk down the street and have to say hello to old patients who smile back with mouths full of a thousand pounds' worth of gold, porcelain and my work that they haven't paid for months after their treatment!' he complains.

He had passed some of his accounts to a collection agency and some cases had come up in the small claims court. 'I never lose in court,' he says, 'but I still have a terrible time getting the money. I have sent in the bailiffs a couple of times. But the chances are it's a widow or a woman whose husband's run off. So they take away her colour telly. That doesn't make you feel good.' His latest collection account on £400 worth of debts, including court costs, had come to £419! I told him about the Continental dentist who had trouble with patients not paying their increased dental charges. To jog their memories he pinned their health service record cards to the wall of his waiting room—and blocked out their names for all to see. When that didn't work, he pasted up statements from the debt-collecting agency he was using. My dentist won't be trying that libellous course here; but he is, on my advice, looking into the possibility of using a factor.

Show them up—and they'll pay up

One of the more outrageous collection methods—expressly forbidden by English law—was practised in South America. In Buenos Aires, where prompt payment of a bill is likely to cast doubt on the customer's sanity, a company calling itself the Eagle Eye Organization hit on a novel way of striking terror into the hearts of debtors. The firm employed a group of seven clean-cut university graduates, dressed them in immaculate top hat, white tie and tails, and sent them off in a vintage car to the houses of clients whose bills were long overdue. The top-hatted visitors were known as 'the gentlemen'. They could neither take money, nor talk to the client. But they did carry bright red brief-cases bearing the words 'sluggish debtors'. On arrival they simply handed over a visiting card. But as all the neighbours knew what was up, the defaulter became an instant laughing stock and shortly afterwards beat a path to the creditor's door, cheque book in hand. Debt collecting folklore has it that a van, advertising boldly on its flanks the legend 'DEBT COLLECTOR', did go the rounds in Britain at one time—but it has never been reliably sighted and no company has ever admitted to using one. Today this would be illegal.

The relative mildness of today's dunning missives is clearly documented in this book. Imagine what it felt like to be a debtor *before* legislation made harassment an offence. A collection letter could—and did—threaten a visit by the debt collector 'by Day and Night'. It might carry the terrifying PS 'WE CANNOT BE HELD RESPONSIBLE FOR DAMAGE CAUSED BY DOGS'. The collector himself was made out to be second cousin to the Wild Man from Borneo, a psychopathic ruffiian who could barely be re-strained and who would be 'unleashed' on debtors who failed to stump up:

> ADVICE OF PASSING TO DEBT COLLECTOR
>
> Your account is now prepared for passing to Mr... Debt Collector.
>
> Arrangements have been made to hand it over in SEVEN DAYS' TIME. A payment immediately and a promise to keep to regular payments would enable us to cancel these arrangements. SO IF YOU WISH TO STOP US TAKING THIS STEP REMIT BY RETURN.
>
> Once your account is in the Debt Collector's hands the matter is beyond our control—he will take whatever steps he considers necessary.
>
> PAYING AT ONCE IS YOUR ONLY REMEDY.

Another letter threatened:

> You will be on the next BLACK LIST to go out to SHOPS, HP Companies, etc. If we find, once the Black List is out, that you owe to two or more creditors a total sum of £50 [nothing dates the letter so much as the pathetic amount out-standing] we will make you BANKRUPT... The only goods we cannot take are your Tools of Trade, wearing apparel and bedding to the value of £20. Really the amount involved is not worth all the trouble it can cause you.
>
> SO LET US HAVE A PAYMENT BY RETURN OF POST.

Some firms send letters designed to put the wind up their debtors by using a feint combined with quasi-legal jargon: 'If we do not hear from you within a week you will be deemed to have admitted liability.' It doesn't really help, though it might spur action, because merely ignoring allegations is not, in law, the same thing as admitting them.

It is more important to be able to prove your debt, by means of letters of contract, invoices, statements, etc. An invoice is sometimes the only bit of evidence submitted by firms that regularly, and successfully, dun clients through the courts.

How to rob a bank (of information)

How do you find how much money you have in your bank account? Phone them up and ask. As identification you'll probably be asked to quote your account number. That's how easy it is to find out how much a rascal has in his account. The account number is the one on the right at the bottom of the cheque. It's illegal, but so, long term, is not paying bills. I wouldn't recommend this course of action for a minute. But you can see the temptation when a client says he's got no money to pay. Picture his face when you tell him, to the point and pence, how much he *really* has in the bank. I think the only other check our so-cautious banks have ever made on my identification when I've rung up for a total on my own current account has been to ask my date of birth. Debtors' dates of birth aren't exactly state secrets, either.

Yesterday's 'foot in the door' debt collector

In the bad old days—or, as some debt collectors would have it, the good old days—debtors were taken to task to a degree that is, today, no longer socially acceptable or legally permissible, thanks to the Administration of Justice Act 1970, Section 40 (see page 4).

But although the form of face-to-face collection is now changed and softened, in accordance with altered mores and sensibilities, the psychology remains the same. I spoke to an 'old school' collector, now comfortably retired, having sold his 'tally' business for a considerable profit.

The tally game grew up in the between-the-war years when people had little money but still needed to buy household items like sheets and blankets and clothes. Outright payment was out of the question, so they paid a small amount each week, often at an extortionate rate of interest if worked out over the year; though it rarely would be, either because the customer was incapable of the necessary arithmetic, or because it was academic—the weekly amount was small, the goods desperately needed and there was no alternative. The tally trick was to keep the payments going indefinitely, by constantly producing tempting new items for the customer to buy. So the collector was also often a door-to-door salesman as well.

My interviewee began in business with a store which invited folk to pay for their clothes as they wore them. Having bought the clothes they were supposed to come in to the shop at regular intervals to pay the instalments. 'But,' he says, 'it didn't work like that. I had to go out and get the money. What happened was that people used to take goods—from many different sources—and eventually they ran into trouble. At some point almost everyone became a slow payer.'

But, according to my friend, only about 5 per cent of people actually did go bad, and the good ones paid for the bad. Thanks to one trick of his trade, the forgetful ones were also made to pay for the bad debts and slow payers: 'If someone owed us money we would put it on the bill of people who never kept a record of how much they'd paid!'

Sometimes what would happen would be that a man would be sold some boots for 10/- on which he was supposed to have paid back 2/- a week. Occasionally the chap would pawn what he'd been sold. Then it was up to the collector to buy the pawn ticket off him and get the goods back much more cheaply. Or even buy the goods off the client, if he still had them, but at a huge discount. It was a way of taking profit at every turn. But so much depended on the personality of the collector. 'Every customer is a potential "DS"—Don't Serve,' says my friend. 'One man's A-call was another man's DS-call; one man could collect and sell goods on top of what he's collected, while another man might not even be able to get the first lot of money owed.'

For slow payers, the approach was to build up a relationship: 'If you're in difficulty I'll try and help you' was the gambit my collector friend used, and he would offer to take a smaller amount than the money owing. It was always important to get people to talk to you, to get to know and, if possible, to like you, said the collector, on the basis that it is harder to give someone a bad time once they know and respect you. In order to win this respect, it was important to look as the debtor expected a collector to look: 'In 1936 I was working for a firm of debt collectors and I always had to go out wearing a buttonhole and hat!'

Another reason for getting close to the customer was that it enabled the collector to get into his home. A typical opener might be: '"I've called to see what's wrong. There must be something wrong; you're not trying to catch me out, you're not a thief or a rogue...." You end up by being a godfather to them.' Once inside the house—known in the trade as 'getting your feet under the table'—it was possible to uncover intimate details of a debtor's work and private life, domestic entanglements, localities of friends and relatives, and his other financial commitments—all of which would be very handy to know if the debtor ever decided to 'go trace'—abscond. 'Even people who had been good customers eventually moved away. They had every intention of letting you have their address, but for one reason or another they'd put it off. And then something came up and they couldn't pay.'

Finding debtors was often no more than a matter of dropping the caretaker a few quid: 'You'd ask him where they'd moved to; or say you'd had their address but had misplaced it. Or you'd pretend to be an insurance man and say they had some money coming to them—or a "big surprise"!'

The easiest type of collection was the HO client or WO client. An HO client was a term collectors used and it meant 'Husband Objects'; for the male purchaser the equivalent was 'Wife Objects'. In other words, the spouse didn't approve of the partner's purchase or method of paying for it. It was easy to dun these folk because the most effective threat possible was to say you'd come back later in the day when their wife/husband was there. It would almost inevitably lead to instant payment.

Embarrassing the slow payer was also virtually guaranteed to have the desired effect: 'I'd go out in the street or stand by the door and raise my voice. I'd say, in the middle of the road: "You have my goods and I want my money". A similar gambit would be to knock on all the neighbours' doors, if the debtor was out, complain that so-and-so was uncontactable, and inevitably the neighbours would draw the conclusion that your prospect was in dire straits.' Violence was always to be shunned; the collector was as liable to get hurt as the debtor, and there was never any promise that the money would be repaid anyway following the fight. But sometimes aggression was called for: 'I've been pushed out of many doors. You don't actually need to insert your foot in the door, the thing is actually to step into the doorway so they can't close it. But some people have managed to close the door in my face. So what I did, I screamed my head off, yelling oh! oh! oh! Immediately they'd open the door because they thought they'd caught my foot in it! I've been hit by more women than men—yes, and I have hit them back.

'One woman smashed me round the face and I spat right in her face. I think I was more embarrassed than she was. Because I had lowered myself to her level.'

The not-so-sweet smell of success

The thought of seriously upsetting the equilibrium of a determined debtor holds an irresistible appeal for many a long-suffering creditor. In 1978 the expression 'financially embarrassed' was given a 'fresh' twist when a firm called London Manhattan launched its 'Smelly collector' scheme on to the unprepared debtor fraternity. A company executive had conceived the 'cough up or throw up' solution after brushing up against an unspeakably filthy and smelly tramp in a Dublin street. The firm advertised the new service in the magazine *Entrepreneur*, owned by an associate company. 'Once we have the pertinent details of an outstanding debt we telephone the debtor, firstly to confirm that a bona fide debt exists and secondly to urge that they send a cheque to our client forthwith.' The response was astonishing: frustrated businessmen creditors flocked to pay the £20 a throw for the services of a Smelly.

The tramp was instructed to stay silent, just to hand the debtor or his secretary a letter for her to pass across. The letter contained details of the debt, the news that the Smelly would not be moving on until a cheque had been received, plus a summary of the Offences Against Persons Act, which warned against forcibly trying to evict the Smelly.

At first the firm used real tramps—but quickly ran into real-life problems. One tramp kept spewing up, while another was forever falling asleep while he waited for the cheques! Though the real tramps never failed to bring home the bacon, it was clear that realistic stand-ins would have to do.

The ersatz tramps went out, faces begrimed, wearing toeless boots and clothes that had been marinated in refuse. (One 'tramp' favoured old cheese, kippers and rotten eggs; another tried rotten fish sewn into the linings of his coat, and finally settled for a vile concoction of specially treated and liquefied compost.)

Even if the boss didn't respond to the Smelly's demand, his staff soon revolted and demanded that the Smelly get his due. The scheme lasted a year, bringing in its wake some useful publicity for the company. It backfired dramatically when a London store owner complained to the police and a Smelly was arrested and charged with insulting behaviour likely to cause a breach of the peace. The Smelly—who explained that the work was bearable only because of his permanently blocked sinuses—was fined £5, ordered to pay £300 costs and bound over to keep the peace for 12 months. So much for a Smelly solution to problem debtors!

12. Paying up—a summing up

By now you will have discovered that there are no rare skills, no sophisticated accounting methods needed to make people pay their debts on time—or sooner. As with any new routine, getting started is the hardest part. You will have learned that it pays dividends to pay close attention to detail in correspondence keeping good clear records, monitoring accounts closely, and staying in constant touch with your customers as much as you can by telephone. In no time you'll be able to switch to 'cruise control' and sit back (but not too far back) while your new, efficient pay machine runs smoothly and you reap the rewards.

Contrary to popular, pusillanimous opinion even a modest-sized business, small trader or a one-man band can learn how to carry the same clout, command the same respect at pay-up time as the big client demands, and gets, as of right. By now you will not be one bit amazed to know that sometimes even the big fish gets into a flap before they get paid, and realize, perhaps too late, that it is an archaic accounting system to blame, or leadership that is too far removed from the nut-chopping end of the business. Blind acceptance of 'traditional pay patterns' in a particular trade has also speeded many an untimely demise.

For all that, making people pay remains a game, a fascinating one at that. But although you will become adept at the various manoeuvres, at keeping steps ahead of your mates in the business jungle; as much as you may come to actually enjoy playing, with your livelihood at stake, you had better learn, and quickly, how to play to win.

Look on this book as a competitors' rulebook. Use it well, but judge it hard. What I said in my first book, *How To Make Money From Antiques* (Blandford, 1980), applies equally to this book: 'Like many another "how to" book, this volume should be judged simply but harshly. If its lessons enable you to recoup the cover price it will have been worth while. The more business-minded will add that an allowance should also be made for the time spent reading it, at a commercial rate per hour. . . .'

Just two pieces of advice in these pages could repay you the cover price a thousandfold. Though you may not be aware of it working for you, recording your mail will greatly enhance your standing in the market place, and mark you out as a serious contender for prompt payment. The other, and more easily noticeable, benefit will be if you can name the exact date by which you want to be paid.

Now that it is a relatively easy matter to sue, there may be a temptation to relax your defences, to slacken your pay posture. Don't do it. If you have not taken the correct steps then you may still lose out in the legal wrangle. And besides, you will waste precious time, sap vital creative energy that is better used making, not chasing, money.

By now, you will probably have guessed that the inspiration for this book was personal anger and frustration. You are right! I got tired of being given the runaround by clients who paid me when it suited them; who, somehow, always seemed to be calling the shots on pay day, even though it had, often as not, been my prompt, professional help that had helped them turn over a profit, or had got them out of trouble. At one time, it got so bad that I formulated The Love Theory of Slow Payment. It runs like this. The more a person enjoys his or her work the more lazy he will be when it comes to getting paid for it. And you don't need to be an Einstein to see that this casual attitude is sure to be catching: paymasters quickly discover whose payments they can paralyse.

Now I believe that you enjoy your work, too. But the fact that you have read this book tells me that you, too, are sick and tired of being penalized on account of the pleasure you take in the work you do. (Those luckless folk whose puritanical streak demands that they suffer for their labours, as well as their sins, have my blessing; but frankly they are beyond help.)

This book has tried to set the record straight on behalf of those who actually enjoy working for a living but do not enjoy working at getting paid. If you follow the simple rules in these pages, you must improve your collection technique—and your cash flow. To that end, I have done my best. Now it's up to you.

Recommended reading

Accounts Collection by Telephone, Protea Management Services, Maidstone.

Administration of Justice Act 1970, Chapter 31, HMSO, London.

Barzman, Sol, *Credit in Early America*, NACM, New York, 1975.

Barzman, Sol, 'The Collection Program: A Practical Guide', NACM, New York, 1979.

Bass, R.M.V., *Credit Management*, Business Books, London, 1979.

Benz, G., *International Trade Credit Management*, Gower Press, Farnborough, 1975.

Bernstein, Lesley, *How to Supervise Credit Accounts*, Gower Press, Farnborough, 1972.

Birks, Michael, 'Small Claims in the County Court: How to Sue and Defend Actions Without a Solicitor,' Lord Chancellor's Office, London, 1978.

Blackstone, Lance, 'How to beat those bad debt manoeuvres', (article), *Entrepreneur-London*, (Magazine), Autumn 1980.

Brock, Luther A., *How to Build Goodwill Through Credit Correspondence*, NACM, New York, 1976.

Brownstone, D.M. and Carruth, G., *Where to Find Business Information: A Worldwide Guide for Everyone Who Needs the Answers to Business Questions*, John Wiley, Chichester, 1979.

Bryan, William H., 'Credit Sleuth: Sherlock Holmes Gives Guidance to the Credit Manager as Investigator', NACM, New York, 1975.

'Business Monitor—M3', *Company Finance*, HMSO, London, 1980.

Butterworth, John, *Debt Collection Letters in Ten Languages*, Gower Press, Farnborough, 1978.

Carson, P.J.B., 'Credit Insurance: An Appreciation', The Chartered Insurance Institute, London, 1978.

'Cash-flow Control'; 'tightening Trade Credit,' Williams & Glyn's Bank Ltd, London, (booklets).

Chapin, Albert F. and Hassett, George E. Jnr, *Credit Collection Principles and Practice*, McGraw-Hill, New York, 1960.

Collection Agencies Association News (monthly journal), Collection Agencies' Association, 5 Mill Street, Bedford.

Collector (monthly journal), American Collectors Association, Inc, Minneapolis.

Correspondence Courses for Examinations for the Institute of Credit Management, The Rapid Results College, Tuition House, 27/37 St. Georges Road, London SW19.

'County Courts to keep their (black lists) of debtors', *Daily Telegraph*, 3 May 1977.

'Credit Clues in Financial Statements', NACM, New York, 1963.

'Credit Control and Debt Collection', (Management Checklist No. 24), British Institute of Management, London, 1981.

'Credit Control for A Small Retailer'; 'Credit Control For A Small Manufacturer'; 'Seeking Company Information'; 'U.K. Sources, Seeking Company Information'; 'International and Foreign Sources,' Department of Industry, London, (booklets).

Credit Insurance and Credit Management, Trade Indemnity Co. Ltd, London.

Credit Management, quarterly journal of the Institute of Credit Management, London.

Credit Management—Video Programme; Credit Management—Audio Programme, Protea Management Services, Maidstone (in-house seminars).

David, R., 'Tackling credit problems', *Financial Times*, 9 January 1976.

Davies, Tom, 'Boom time for dunners', *Sunday Telegraph*, 14 December 1975.

Davies, Tom, 'How not to get dunned', *Sunday Times*, 27 February 1972.

Documentary Operations, Swiss Bank Corporation, Zurich, 1979.

Dun & Bradstreet Newssheets, Good Relations (Corporate Affairs) Ltd, 28 Bedford Square, London WC1.

Dun & Bradstreet Register, The (updated weekly), Dun & Bradstreet, London.

ECGD Services, revised edition, Export Credits Guarantee Department & Central Office of Information, London, 1975.

Edwards, H. (ed.), *Credit Management Handbook*, Gower Press, Farnborough, 1976.

Edwards, H., *Export Credit*, Shaws Linton Publications, Wantage, 1980.

England, Olga K., 'There's no business like your business', *Over 21*, January 1980.

'Fair Deal: A Shoppers' Guide,' Office of Fair Trading, London.

Feld, Lipman G., *Bad Checks and Fraudulent Identity: How to Protect Yourself*, NACM, New York, 1978.

Garbutt, Douglas, 'Abolish trade credit', *Accountant*, 11 January 1973.

Gatenby, J.K. (ed.), *Parke's Collection of Debts*, Oyez, London, 1976.

'Guidance for Credit Reference Agencies'; 'Extortionate Credit—New Safeguards for Consumers'; 'The Consumer Credit Public Register'; 'Regulated and Exempt Agreements'; 'Are You a Credit Broker?'; 'A Limitation on Fees'; 'A Guide to the Consumer Credit Tables'; 'Low-Cost Credit Exemption, Fair Deal on Credit, Equal Liability'; 'Buying or Selling on Credit—Who's Responsible If Things Go Wrong?', Office of Fair Trading, London (booklets).

'Guide for UK Exporters,' National Westminster Bank Ltd, London, 1980.

'A Handbook for Exporters,' National Westminster Bank Ltd, London.

Hennessy, Elizabeth, *The Entrepreneurs*, Scope Books, Newbury, 1980.

'Here's a new debt collection business that really stinks!' (article), *Entrepreneur-London* (magazine), Winter 1978.

Hoffman, Charles H., 'How to Improve Collections Without Really Trying', NACM, New York, 1977.

Hoffman, Charles H., *The True Nature of Discounts and Interest Charges*, NACM, New York, 1980.

Hutson, Thomas Guybon, and Butterworth, John, *Management of Trade Credit*, 2nd edn, Gower Press, Farnborough, 1974.

'ICI sets the pace in shortening credit', *Investor's Chronicle*, 11 June 1976.

'Industrial Performance Analysis,' Throgmorton Publications, 1975 (booklet).

'Inter-Credit Tele-Prompter', Inter-Credit International Ltd, New Barnet.

Jacobson, Philip, 'Last stop, Carey Street', *Sunday Times*, 20 November 1966.

Karrer, Hans, *The Elements of Credit Insurance*, Pitman, London, 1957.

Kempthorne, Brian (ed.), *Croner's Reference Book for Exporters*, Croner Publications Ltd, London, 1980.

Kirkman, Patrick, R.A., *Modern Credit Management*, Allen & Unwin, London, 1977.

'Legal Action in Collecting Accounts'; 'Techniques of Account Collection'; 'Commercial Debt Collection', Inter-Credit International Ltd, New Barnet, (booklets).

Lewellen, W. G. and Johnson, R. W., 'Better way to monitor accounts receivable', *Harvard Business Review*, May–June, 1972.

Lewis, Mel, *How to Make Money from Antiques*, Blandford, Poole, 1980.

'Licensing', Office of Fair Trading, London, 1980.

Lowe, Robert and Woodroffe, Geoffrey, *Consumer Law and Practice*, Sweet & Maxwell, London, 1980.

Mayo, Owen G. (ed.), *Consumer Credit Control*, Gower Press, Farnborough, 1971.

Mogano, M., *How to Start And Run Your Own Business*, Graham & Trotman, London, 1980.

'Mr. Smelly the debt-collector gets a whiff of failure', *Daily Telegraph*, 19 February 1980.

O'Neill, Cooke, 'Credit and Collections', NACM, New York.

Procter, Gordon, 'How to prevent disaster when a client collapses', *Campaign*, 25 April 1980.

Raven, B., 'Towards profitable credit control', *Accountancy*, August 1973.

Rock, Paul, *Making People Pay*, Routledge & Kegan Paul, London, 1973.

'Service charges—help or hindrance on past due accounts', *Credit & Financial Management*, March, 1970.

Significant Aspects of Credit Management, Canadian Credit Institute, Ontario, 1974.

Simpson, Colin, 'Why Carey Street is paved with gold', *Sunday Times*, 26 April 1981.

Stanley, Oliver, 'How to make the most of a bad debt', *Sunday Times*, 11 December 1966.

Stanley, Oliver, 'Insuring that it's all very much to your credit', *Sunday Times*, 3 December 1967.

'Starting Your Own Business'; 'Making a Small Business Bigger,' Lloyds Bank Ltd, London (booklets).

Sullivan, Lorana, 'Nasty gifts by parcel post', *Sunday Times*, 31 August 1975.

'The way debtors are dunned', *Sunday Times*, 24 August 1969.

Thomas, Doina, 'Debt collecting with the female touch', *Financial Times*, 15 November 1972.

Timson, Gordon, 'Would you swap for cash?', *Entrepreneur-London*, (Magazine), Spring 1979.

Ward, Christopher, *How to Complain*, Pan, London, 1980.

Ward, Christopher, *Our Cheque is in the Post: A Book of Excuses*, Secker & Warburg, 1980.

Watson, Ian, 'Firms get tough over bad debts', *Sunday Telegraph*, 18 January 1976.

Welshams, M.T., 'Using credit for profit-making', *Harvard Business Review*, January–February 1967.

Wey, Frank W., 'Measuring the Impact of Past-Due Accounts on the Receivables Portfolio,' (articles), Credit Research Foundation, Inc., Lake Success, NY, 1974.

Wheatcroft, Patience, 'If foreigners won't pay', *Sunday Times*, 17 September 1978.

Useful addresses

Alex Lawrie Factors, Beaumont House, Beaumont Road, Banbury, Oxfordshire.

ATP International Credit and Business Information and Commercial Collections, 54/58 High Street, Edgware, Middlesex.

Barclays Factoring Ltd, PO Box 9, Paddington House, Basingstoke, Hants.

British Mercantile Group of Companies, The, Sidcup House, 12–18 Station Road, Sidcup, Kent TA15 7EH.

Credit Factoring International Ltd, Smith House, PO Box 50, Elmwood Avenue, Feltham, Middlesex TW13 7QD.

Credit for Industry Ltd, United Dominion House, Eastcheap, London EC3.

Dun & Bradstreet Ltd, London (Head Office), 26/32 Clifton Street, London EC2P 2LY.

Extel Statistical Services Ltd (business information), 37–45 Paul Street, London EC2

Global Credit Management, 27 Buckingham Gardens, Edgware, Middlesex.

H&H Factors Ltd, 46–48 Wellesley Road, Croydon, Surrey.

Inter-Credit International Ltd, Inter-Credit House, 205/207 Crescent Road, New Barnet, Herts EN4 8SW.

Interdebt, Granada Credit Collection Ltd, Granada House, Gabriels Hill, Maidstone, Kent.

International Factors Group, 4 Vigo Street, London W1.

Mercantile Credit Company Ltd, PO Box No 75, Elizabethan House, Great Queen Street, London WC2B 5DB.

Sales Ledger Control Services, Sidcup House, Station Road, Sidcup, Kent.

Helpful organizations

American Collectors Association, Inc., 4040 West 70th Street, Box 35106, Minneapolis, Mn 55435, USA.

Association of British Factors Ltd, The, Markbys Moore Avenue, London Wall, London EC2Y 5HE.

British Export Houses Association, 69 Cannon Street, London EC4.

British Institute of Management, Management House, Parker Street, London WC2.

Chartered Insurance Institute, 20 Aldermanbury, London EC2.

City of Westminster Chamber of Commerce, The, Mitre House, 177 Regent Street, London W1.

Credit Agencies Association, 5 Mill Street, Bedford MK40 3EU.

Credit Protection Association Ltd, The, Westgate House, 47/55 The Vale, London W3.

Credit Research Foundation, Inc, 3000 Marcus Avenue, Lake Success, NY 11042, USA.

Department of Trade, Export Services Promotion Division, Export House, 50 Ludgate Hill, London EC4.

ECGD (Export Credit Guarantee Department), regional offices in Glasgow, Manchester, Birmingham, Belfast, Leeds, Cambridge, Bristol, Croydon and London.

HM Customs & Excise, Information Office, King's Beam House, Mark Lane, London EC3.

Inland Revenue, Somerset House, London WC2.

Institute of Credit Management, ICM House, High Street, Ascot, Berkshire SL5 7HU.

International Chamber of Commerce, Centre Point, 103 New Oxford Street, London WC1.

Law Society, The, 113 Chancery Lane, London WC2.

London Chamber of Commerce and Industry, 69–75 Cannon Street, London EC4.

National Association of Credit Management, 475 Park Avenue South, New York, NY 10016, U.S.A.

National Federation of Self-Employed and Small Businesses Ltd, 32 St Annes Road West, Lytham St Annes, Lancs FY8 1NY.

National Union of Small Shopkeepers, Western Buildings, Theatre Square, Nottingham.

Small Firms Information Service, 8 Bulstrode Street, London W1 (or dial 100 and ask for Freefone 2444).

UAPT (United Association for the Protection of Trade Ltd), Zodiac House, 163 London Road, Croydon CR9 2RP.

Union of Independent Companies, 3 Lincoln Street, London SE3.

Index